Games to Play with Toddlers

KT-119-601

by Jackie Silberg

Illustrations by Linda Greigg

Brilliant Publications

We hope you have enjoyed using this book. There are two
other books available in the series, also written by Jackie
Silberg:

Games to Play with Babies   ISBN   1 897675 54 2
Games to Play with Two Year Olds   ISBN   1 897675 56 9

Published by Brilliant Publications, The Old School Yard, Leighton
Road, Northall, Dunstable LU6 2HA

Originally published in 1993 by Gryphon House, Inc, 10726 Tucker
Street, Beltsville, MD 20705, USA

Written by Jackie Silberg
Illustrated by Linda Greigg
Cover photo by Martyn Chillmaid

Printed in Malta by Interprint Ltd

© Jackie Silberg 1993
ISBN 1 897675 55 0

First published in the UK in 1999
10 9 8 7 6 5 4 3 2 1

Table of Contents

Teddy Bear Games

Kitchen Games

Laughing and Having Fun Games

Car Games

Special Bonding Games

Bath and Dressing Games

Finger and Toe Games

From the author

Toddlers are a joy to be around. They are inquisitive and thrive on exploration and creativity. Social interaction with loving adults helps toddlers develop trust and emotional security. When toddlers feel safe to express their energy and creative potential, their development thrives. Games are a natural way for parents and other caregivers to interact with toddlers in a positive way. Since the beginning of time, parents have played games with toddlers. You may find a familiar game or rhyme in this book that you had forgotten about.

Together, adults and children have played and enjoyed all the games in this book. Originating from a variety of cultures and ethnic backgrounds, the games were carefully selected for this age range.

I can't think of anything more delightful than playing with a toddler. Enjoy yours!

The age range given for each activity is an approximation. Remember that each child develops at his or her own pace. Use your knowledge of each individual child as the best judgment as to whether an activity is appropriate.

Guidelines for growth

Walks independently
Walks up and down stairs holding an adult's hand
Holds two small objects in one hand
Jumps in place
Kicks a large ball
Throws a small ball overhand
Recognizes familiar people
Scribbles on paper
Stacks three to six blocks
Turns knobs
Finds objects of the same colour, shape and size
Points to distant, interesting objects outdoors
Turns towards a family member whose name is spoken
Understands and follows a simple direction
Notices sounds made by a clock, bell, whistle
Responds rhythmically to music with her whole body
Carries out instructions that include two steps

Language and cognitive skills

Jabbers with expression
Identifies pictures in a book
Uses single words meaningfully
Names objects when asked, "What's this?"
Uses twenty or more words
Names at least twenty-five familiar objects
Gestures to make his wants known
Names toys
Uses words to make wants known
Combines two different words
Tries to sing
Speaks in simple sentences
Finds familiar objects
Fits objects into containers
Turns two to three pages of a book at a time

Points to pictures in a book
Remembers where objects belong
Obtains a toy using a stick or a string

Self-concept skills
Demands personal attention
Points to parts of his body when identified
Insists on helping to feed herself
Names parts of a doll's body
Claims objects as his own
Refers to herself by name
Pulls on socks and mittens
Eats with a spoon
Drinks from a cup
Attempts to wash himself
Offers a toy but does not release it
Plays independently around another child
Enjoys short walks
Asks for food and water when needed

Growing and Learning Games

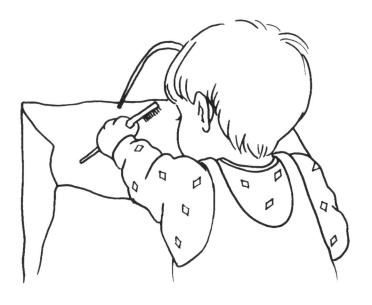

Colour games

◆ The first step in learning to identify colours is matching them.

◆ Sit on the floor with your child. Zoom a toy car back and forth. Choose a red or blue car.

◆ After you and your toddler have played for a while, take out a car of a different colour and play with that one.

◆ Next, take two sheets of paper the same colour as the cars. Put the paper on the floor and the cars on the matching paper.

◆ Take a car off and ask your child to put the car on the matching paper. As you play this game, always name the colour to which you are referring.

◆ Consistently playing this game will develop your child's matching skills.

WHAT YOUR TODDLER WILL LEARN:
About colours

Box games

◆ Boxes can provide hours of enjoyment for young children.

◆ Gather together several small toys and plastic containers. Give your child a large box. Encourage her to drop the toys into the box and dump them out again.

◆ Cut out shapes (circles, squares, triangles) from the top of a box. Give your toddler the shapes and see if she can fit them into the correct holes.

◆ Give your toddler several boxes of different sizes. Help her learn how to stack the boxes. She will soon understand to put the largest on the bottom. The same boxes can be used for nesting.

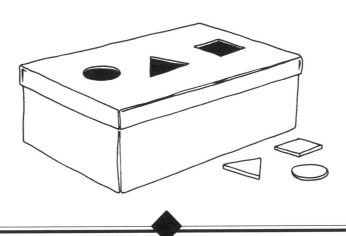

WHAT YOUR TODDLER WILL LEARN:
About shapes

Outdoor fun

◆ Take your toddler outside and discover all kinds of wonderful things:

- Feel the wind in your hair.
- Feel the raindrops on your face.
- Smell a flower.
- Watch a butterfly.
- Hold a worm in your hands.
- Lie in the grass and look at the clouds.
- Squish your toes in the mud.

◆ More things to do:

- Crunch an autumn leaf.
- Jump in a pile of leaves.
- Care for plants and watch them grow.
- Taste fresh fruits and vegetables from the garden.
- Taste a snowflake.

WHAT YOUR TODDLER WILL LEARN:

Nature appreciation

Clip the clothespeg

◆ Remove the lid from a large tin or similar container that has no sharp or ragged metal edges.

◆ Show your toddler how to slip a clothespeg on to the rim of the tin.

◆ Give your child several clothespegs to put on the tin, then show her how to drop the clothespegs into the tin.

◆ Toddlers are fascinated with this game, which is excellent for hand–eye coordination.

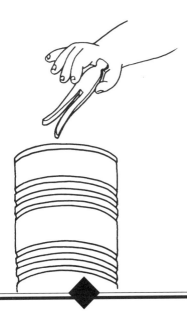

WHAT YOUR TODDLER WILL LEARN:
Coordination

Can you do this?

This is a great game for a grumpy toddler

◆ Holding your toddler in your arms, stand in front of a large mirror and say, "Look at the pretty baby."

◆ Make animated faces in the mirror while the baby watches. He will imitate you.

◆ Hold up your child's arm and say, "See the baby's arm?" Do this with different parts of his body.

◆ Kiss your toddler. Kiss your reflection. Blink your eyes. Play peek-a-boo.

WHAT YOUR TODDLER WILL LEARN:

Imitation

Happy–sad puppets

◆ Find two wooden spoons. Draw a happy face on one and a sad face on the other, using felt-tip markers.

◆ Sit in a chair with your toddler on your lap.

◆ Hold up the happy face and say cheerful things: "Oh, what a nice day," or "You are such a good boy."

◆ Hold up the sad face and change the tone of your voice accordingly. Sounds like "boo hoo" and "waaa waaa" are favourites of young children.

◆ Ask your toddler if she wants the happy voice or the sad voice. Give her a spoon and encourage her to say something.

◆ Respond with great enthusiasm to whatever sounds she makes.

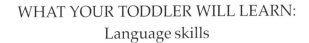

WHAT YOUR TODDLER WILL LEARN:
Language skills

Body part game

◆ When a young child is beginning to name the parts of his body, play this game.

◆ Touch your ears, saying to the child, "I am touching my ears. Can you touch your ears?"

◆ Give your toddler time and repeat the question if need be. If he is keeping up, use words that he doesn't usually hear, such as elbows, chin, ankles, back, etc., and encourage him to say the words, too.

◆ If your child touches a new part of his body, name that part as you imitate him.

◆ Songs that name parts of the body will reinforce this game. "Looby Loo" and "Hokey cokey" are two excellent songs.

WHAT YOUR TODDLER WILL LEARN:
Language skills

Building blocks

◆ Sit on the floor with your toddler.

◆ Put down one block and say, "I am putting one block on the floor."

◆ Add a block and say, "I am putting two blocks on the floor."

◆ Repeat with a third block.

◆ Knock down the tower. Urge the baby to rebuild it, if necessary with your help.

◆ As the child's coordination increases, the tower will get taller.

WHAT YOUR TODDLER WILL LEARN:
Coordination

Personal puzzles

◆ Give your toddler a large sheet of construction paper or similarly sturdy paper.

◆ Give him a crayon to draw with.

◆ Cover the art work with transparent contact paper.

◆ Cut the paper into two or three pieces, depending on your child's development.

◆ Give him the puzzle and help him put it together.

◆ Make puzzles out of sandwiches and slices of cheese.

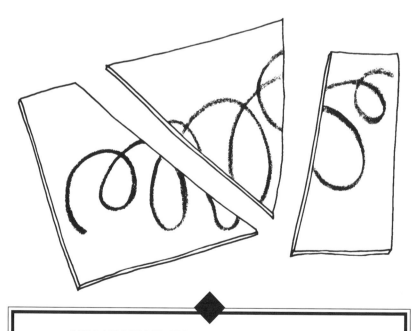

WHAT YOUR TODDLER WILL LEARN:
To put puzzles together

Beanbag fun

◆ Beanbags are excellent toys for young children. They are safe, soft, and stimulate creativity.

◆ Think of all the things to do with a beanbag while playing with your toddler:

- Throw them.
- Stack them.
- Put them on your head.
- Put them on your back.
- Put them on your stomach.
- Lie on your back with your feet in the air and balance a beanbag on each foot.
- Drop them into containers.

WHAT YOUR TODDLER WILL LEARN:
Creativity

Make-believe house

◆ Make a tent or a playhouse for your child. Drape a sheet over a card table or the backs of two or more chairs to make a simple tent.

◆ If you want more detail, make walls and a roof out of felt for the card table. Decorate the walls.

◆ Pretend that the tent is a cave, an aeroplane, a train, a spaceship or a house.

◆ Take a pillow, blanket and stuffed toy inside your make-believe house.

WHAT YOUR TODDLER WILL LEARN:
Creativity

Blocks can be anything

This activity encourages creativity

◆ Help your child learn to pretend with blocks.

◆ Take a block in your hand and push it along the floor. Tell the child, "Here is Susie, driving in the car."

◆ Add other phrases to expand your block story, such as, "Beep beep, look out, you cars!" or "Time to stop for the light."

◆ Encourage your toddler to use the blocks in other imaginative ways. Pretend the blocks are two different people carrying on a conversation, for example.

WHAT YOUR TODDLER WILL LEARN:
Imaginative play

Hello! Who's there?

◆ Get a toy telephone, one that your child can play with on her own or with you.

◆ Say, "Ding-a-ling, ding-a-ling." Pretend the phone is ringing and answer it.

◆ As you are talking to the imaginary person (someone the baby knows, like grandparents or a friend), also talk to the baby. For example, say, "Hello, Grandpa." Then say to your child, "It's your grandpa." Talk about a special activity, a visit, a meal or maybe plans for the day. Be sure your toddler will understand the topic.

◆ Be sure to say "Good-bye" and hang up the phone.

◆ Give the phone to your child and encourage her to have an imaginary conversation.

WHAT YOUR TODDLER WILL LEARN:
Language skills

Get the object

◆ Place one object that your baby can recognize, like a toy or familiar household item, on the other side of the room.

◆ Ask your toddler to bring it to you: "Please go and fetch the doll."

◆ When he has retrieved the object, reinforce this feat with a compliment and a big hug.

◆ Increase the challenge by adding more objects. For example, put a hat, a shoe and a block across the room and tell your toddler to get the shoe.

◆ Ask your child to bring other objects from around the room.

◆ An even more challenging variation is to hide the object —under a chair, around a corner, behind a cushion— and have your toddler look for it.

WHAT YOUR TODDLER WILL LEARN:
Language skills

Word book

◆ Toddlers are developing their vocabulary every day. Sometimes they say words and sometimes they just think them, but they understand many.

◆ Select several of your toddler's favourite words and find pictures to match them: car, doggie, etc.

◆ Show the pictures to your child and ask her about them.

◆ Paste each picture on a separate sheet of paper and make a book for her.

◆ Your toddler will love looking at the book with you as well as by herself.

WHAT YOUR TODDLER WILL LEARN:
Language skills

It's in the bag

◆ Select two or three simple, familiar objects like keys, a comb, ball, toothbrush.

◆ Show each item to your child. Let him hold it in his hand. Talk about the way that it feels, and name it. Put it into a paper bag.

◆ Ask your toddler to reach into the bag and remove something.

◆ See whether he can tell you what it is.

◆ Ask him to retrieve a particular object. He will have to feel around inside in order to find the right one.

◆ If this seems too difficult for your toddler, start with one object and slowly graduate to two and three.

WHAT YOUR TODDLER WILL LEARN:
Problem-solving skills

Toy transfer game

◆ Place two large containers on opposite sides of a room.

◆ Fill one container with small toys.

◆ Have a third container that is easy to carry, such as a basket with a handle.

◆ Show your toddler how to load the toys from the full container into the basket, carry them across the room and dump them into the empty container.

◆ She may have to make more than one trip to empty the toy basket. When it is empty, say, "All gone!"

◆ Repeat the activity. Say, "All gone!" whenever she empties a basket.

◆ As you repeat this game a few times, try using the words "empty" and "full".

◆

WHAT YOUR TODDLER WILL LEARN:
About empty and full

Matching shapes

◆ Cut holes in the top of a box or the plastic lid of a coffee tin to match the shapes of household objects.

◆ Choose round, triangular or square objects, for example, cotton reels, plastic hair rollers, biscuit cutters.

◆ Place the box or tin in front of your toddler and let him explore it with his hands.

◆ Drop one object through the correct hole. Then give your toddler the same object and guide his hand to the correct place.

◆ Repeat this activity until you use all the objects.

◆ Let your toddler experiment on his own.

WHAT YOUR TODDLER WILL LEARN:
Matching skills

Doll play

◆ Following directions is difficult for toddlers because it requires listening and doing something at the same time. Doll play is a good way to practise this skill.

◆ Give your toddler her favourite doll or stuffed animal and ask her to identify the parts of its body: "Where's the doll's head, ears, legs, tummy," and so forth.

◆ Suggest she do specific things with the doll:

- Brush the doll's hair.
- Tickle the doll's tummy.
- Wash the doll's face.
- Brush the doll's teeth.

◆ Not only will your toddler improve her listening skills, but she will practise nurturing behaviour that she has experienced as your child.

WHAT YOUR TODDLER WILL LEARN:

Listening skills

Fit the pieces

◆ This is a game that your toddler will enjoy playing over and over.

◆ Collect several biscuit cutters. Try to get shapes that your toddler will recognize, like animals or holiday figures and objects.

◆ Start by tracing around one biscuit cutter with a marker. Give your toddler the biscuit cutter that matches the shape you drew. Show him how they fit together.

◆ After tracing several biscuit cutters and showing how they match, give your toddler two biscuit cutters and one tracing and see whether he can choose the matching biscuit cutter.

◆ Once he understands, add another tracing and another biscuit cutter.

WHAT YOUR TODDLER WILL LEARN:
Matching skills

Magic mud

◆ Mix a box of cornflour with enough water to achieve the consistency of bread dough.

◆ Say to your toddler, "Let's be very quiet and watch some magic."

◆ If you roll the mixture, it forms a ball. If you let it rest, it dissolves to liquid.

◆ Sing to the tune of "Row, row, row your boat" as you roll the cornflour.

> *Take some magic mud,*
> *And roll it in a ball.*
> *Now we will sit so very still,*
> *And watch it disappear.*

WHAT YOUR TODDLER WILL LEARN:
Observation skills

Watch the birds eat

◆ Watching birds is fascinating and fun to do with your toddler.

◆ Make a simple bird-feeder using a pine cone: spread the pine cone with peanut butter, then roll it in birdseed. NOTE: you should do this yourself if your child has a nut allergy.

◆ Hang the pine cone near a window where it can be easily observed.

◆ Talk with your child about what birds eat and where they find food.

◆ You will be amazed at the different birds that come to your feeder. You will have many opportunities to talk about the colour, size, language and other aspects of the birds.

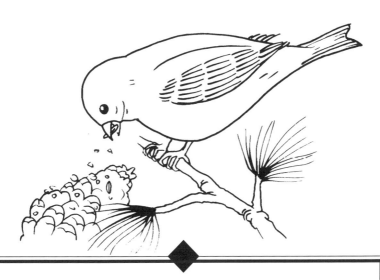

WHAT YOUR TODDLER WILL LEARN:
Observation skills

Do what I do

◆ Play a game of imitation with your toddler.

◆ Perform different actions and encourage your child to imitate you: wave your hands, wiggle your fingers, stamp your feet, pretend to be asleep.

◆ Let your toddler do something while you imitate him. At first, you may have to make suggestions. Suggest easy movements like waving bye-bye or clapping hands.

◆ Adapt this activity to jobs around the house and garden like raking leaves, dusting, sweeping.

WHAT YOUR TODDLER WILL LEARN:
Imitation

Opening jars

◆ Gather together plastic jars with lids small enough for little hands to remove.

◆ Put a colourful and interesting toy in each jar. Close the lid.

◆ Give your toddler one jar at a time for her to remove the lid and retrieve the toy.

◆ Your child will want to practise this game over and over.

WHAT YOUR TODDLER WILL LEARN:
Coordination

Unwrapping game

◆ Wrap a ball or a toy in colourful paper.

◆ Show the wrapped toy to your toddler and ask, "What do you think is inside?"

◆ Give the wrapped toy to your child to remove the paper.

◆ This is difficult for a young child, and he will be enthralled by the effort. The sound of the paper might excite him more than the toy itself.

◆ Gather several kinds of paper: tissue, foil, wrapping paper and newspaper.

◆ Take the toy that your child unwrapped and wrap it in another kind of paper while he watches.

◆ Let him unwrap again. Continue until he tires of the game.

WHAT YOUR TODDLER WILL LEARN:
Coordination

Fishing

◆ Remove the top from a cardboard box. Place several metal bottle tops—painted bright colours, if possible— in the box.

◆ Tie a piece of string to a stick and a magnet to the free end of the string.

◆ Show your child how to "fish" in the box, catching the bottle tops with the magnet.

◆ If you have painted the bottle tops, direct your child to fish for a certain colour.

◆ After you have caught all the bottle caps, count how many you have, then start all over again.

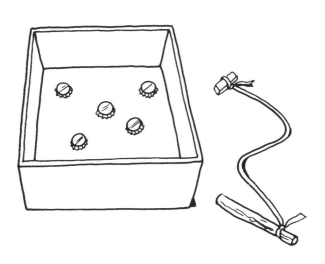

WHAT YOUR TODDLER WILL LEARN:
Coordination

Puzzle pieces

◆ Gather together cardboard party decorations like Halloween characters, birthday scenes, Valentines.

◆ Cut each decoration in two, like pieces of a puzzle.

◆ Cut so that the pieces are all different shapes.

◆ Give your toddler one piece. Mix the others up and spread them out on the floor.

◆ Talk with your toddler about the piece in her hand—its colour, shape and other features.

◆ Help her find the matching piece. Continue playing the game with another piece. Keep helping her until she plays by herself.

WHAT YOUR TODDLER WILL LEARN:
To put puzzles together

All about me

◆ Take photographs of your toddler throughout the day.

◆ Paste the photographs on heavy paper, punch a hole in each sheet of paper and attach with metal rings to make a book.

◆ Look at the pictures with your toddler and talk about the different things that she does during the day: getting dressed, eating, playing, going outside, taking a bath.

◆ As you go through the day, show your toddler the picture that relates to each activity.

◆ You will soon see your child looking at the book herself and getting much pleasure from it.

WHAT YOUR TODDLER WILL LEARN:
Language skills

Turning on lights

◆ Toddlers spend a good part of the day acquiring skills to help them become self-sufficient.

◆ One skill they love to practise is turning switches off and on.

◆ If you have a light in your house that turns off and on with a pull of some kind, extend the pull so that your toddler can reach it.

◆ Be sure that the extension is safe for your toddler.

◆ Imagine the thrill and pride that your child feels when she turns the light off and on all by herself.

WHAT YOUR TODDLER WILL LEARN:

Independence

Hippity hoppity

◆ Recite the poem, using your hand to play out the actions:

> *Hippity hoppity hippity hay,*
> *Five little bunnies went out to play.*
> *("hop" five fingers)*
> *Hippity hoppity hippity hay,*
> *One little bunny hopped away.*
> *(hide your hand behind your back)*
> *Hippity hoppity hippity hay,*
> *Four little bunnies went out to play.*
> *("hop" four fingers)*

◆ Repeat the poem, each time reducing the number of bunnies—and fingers—by one.

◆ Then say,

> *Hippity hoppity hippity ho,*
> *Where did all the bunnies go?*

◆ Talk about where the bunnies might have gone—to take a nap, to look for food, etc.

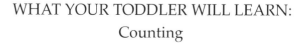

WHAT YOUR TODDLER WILL LEARN:
Counting

Twos

◆ Toddlers are not ready to count or recognize numbers, but they can understand the basic concept of "two".

◆ Help your child begin to understand this concept by pointing out many things that come in pairs:

- two shoes
- two socks
- two hands
- two feet
- two ears

◆ In your conversation, use the word "two" whenever possible: "Look at those two flowers."

◆ Give your toddler things in "twos": "Here are two spoons," or "Here are two toys."

WHAT YOUR TODDLER WILL LEARN:
Counting

In the bag

◆ This game develops the thinking process. The child hears the word, makes an association, then finds the object.

◆ Get a large shopping bag.

◆ Ask your toddler to bring you things to put into the bag.

◆ Ask for one object at a time, letting your child put each one into the bag. Always say "thank you" to your child.

◆ Select objects that your toddler can reach and bring to you on her own, such as a favourite toy, cutlery, a blanket, a towel or a toothbrush.

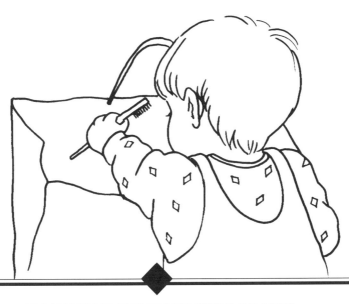

WHAT YOUR TODDLER WILL LEARN:
Problem-solving skills

Which one?

◆ Sit on the floor with your toddler

◆ Find three containers. (Tins or margarine tubs work very nicely.) Put a small toy under one of the containers while your toddler watches.

◆ Move the containers around slowly, changing their positions while your child watches.

◆ Let your toddler pick the one he thinks hides the toy.

◆ If your child does not understand, pick up the container and show him the toy. Show him that the other containers do not hide a toy.

◆ Play the game showing your child the answer until he understands and can play the game without help.

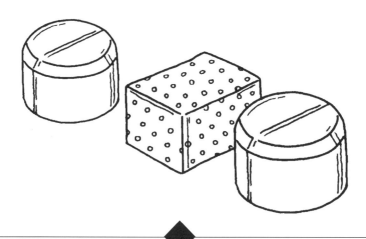

WHAT YOUR TODDLER WILL LEARN:
Problem-solving skills

Whee! Over the book!

◆ Lay a small book on the floor.

◆ Show your toddler how to jump over the book.

◆ Sing to the tune of "Here we go 'round the mulberry bush":

> *I am jumping over the book,*
> *Over the book, over the book.*
> *I am jumping over the book,*
> *See me jumping now, WHEE!!!!*

◆ Hold your child's arms and sing the song again. On the words "See me jumping now, WHEE!!" lift him up and over the book. Replace the word "me" with your child's name.

◆ Repeat again and again. Once the child can jump alone, replace the book with a new, larger object.

◆ Try other actions like hopping, flying, swimming, going backwards, etc.

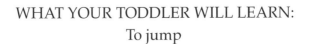

WHAT YOUR TODDLER WILL LEARN:
To jump

Follow the leader

This is a game the entire family can play

◆ Make a straight path on the floor with newspapers, taping them into place.

◆ Show the path to your toddler and say, "This is the long path you can walk on."

◆ Demonstrate how to walk on the path using both arms to balance.

◆ Ask your toddler to follow you on the path. If she doesn't understand, hold her hand to guide her. If you have to help your child, you will need another person to lead.

◆ If your toddler does well, make a more difficult path that curves or winds in and out of other rooms.

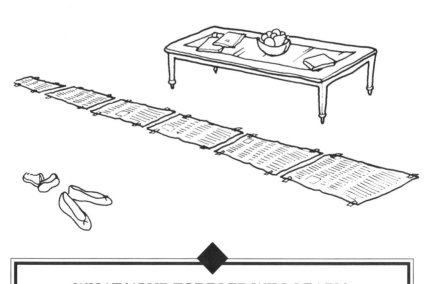

WHAT YOUR TODDLER WILL LEARN:

Balance

The sound game

◆ Put into several film canisters things that make a variety of sounds, such as a coin, a button, a cotton wool ball, popcorn or sand. NOTE: Be sure that the canister lids are fastened securely and that your toddler cannot remove them.

◆ Show your toddler how to shake the canisters. Give her time to shake them and listen to all the sounds.

◆ Pick two canisters, one that makes a loud sound and the other a soft sound. Shake the soft one and say, "Soft...shhh," in a very soft voice. Shake the louder one and say, in a loud voice, "Loud."

◆ Ask your toddler to shake the soft one and then the loud one.

◆ As she holds the canisters, she will become aware that one is heavier, one lighter. Although she is too young to understand this concept, she is acquiring a feel for differences in weight.

◆ Try using the words "noisy" and "quiet" instead of "soft" and "loud".

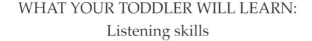

WHAT YOUR TODDLER WILL LEARN:
Listening skills

Spinning around

◆ Cut pictures from magazines of things familiar to your toddler—animals, people, toys, etc.

◆ Get a kitchen cabinet turntable or something similar that spins around.

◆ Put the pictures on the turntable (you may have to tape them down) and spin it.

◆ While you spin the turntable, say, "One, two, three, spin."

◆ When the turntable stops, point to the picture in front of your child and talk to him about it.

◆ Continue playing the game. If the same picture stops in front of your toddler, talk about it again.

◆ Let your child try to spin the turntable.

◆ This kind of interaction will not only build a child's vocabulary but a special relationship between you and your child.

WHAT YOUR TODDLER WILL LEARN:

Language skills

First reading game

◆ Cut pictures out of catalogues and magazines. Paste the pictures onto cards.

◆ Show a picture to your toddler and talk to him about it. Talk about the colour, the shape, how it is used, etc.

◆ Give the card to your toddler and name the object, for example, "shoe".

◆ Ask your toddler to give you the "shoe" picture.

◆ Once he understands, introduce another picture card. Then, when you ask him for a picture, he will have to choose between two.

WHAT YOUR TODDLER WILL LEARN:
Language skills

Walking on shapes

◆ Use wide, sturdy tape to create shapes on the floor, like circles, squares, triangles and zigzags.

◆ Show your toddler how to walk on the tape. Start with the circle.

◆ Hold your toddler's hand and walk together. As you walk around and around, sing to the tune of "Twinkle, twinkle, little star".

> *We are walking on the circle,*
> *Tra, la, la, la, la, la, la.*
> *We are walking on the circle,*
> *Tra, la, la, la, la, la, la.*

◆ Go to the next shape and sing the song again.

> *We are walking on the square,*
> *Tra, la, la, la, la, la, la.*
> *We are walking on the square,*
> *Tra, la, la, la, la, la, la.*

◆ After you have walked on all the shapes, try other ways to move across them: walk backwards, sideways, on your tiptoes. Try to hop, jump, crawl and march on the shapes.

WHAT YOUR TODDLER WILL LEARN:
About shapes

Teddy Bear Games

Where's the bear?

◆ Tie one end of a long string around your child's favourite teddy bear and hide the bear in a cupboard.

◆ Close the cupboard door, trail the string out under the door and run it around, over and under furniture and other objects in the room.

◆ Say to your toddler, "Let's find Teddy."

◆ Help her hold the string and follow it to the bear.

◆ Your child will absolutely love this game. Play it again, and as you follow the string, describe where you are going, for example, "The string is behind the chair; the string is under the rug," etc.

◆ When you find the teddy bear, give him a big hug and say, "Oh, Teddy, we're so glad we found you!"

WHAT YOUR TODDLER WILL LEARN:
Concentration

Teddy cave

◆ Enjoy this fingerplay with your toddler, acting out the story with your hand:

> *Here is a cave.*
> *(bend your fingers into your palm)*
> *Inside is Mr Teddy Bear.*
> *(wiggle your thumb, then fold it under the bent fingers)*
> *Oh, please Teddy, won't you come out?*
> *(tap on the cave with the index finger of your other hand)*
> *Here he comes to get some fresh air.*
> *(pop out your thumb)*

◆ Repeat the rhyme, guiding her fingers through the motions.

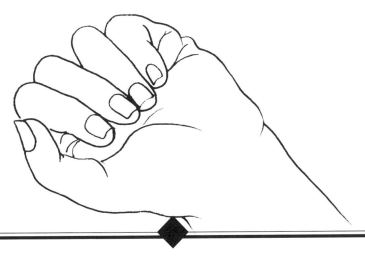

WHAT YOUR TODDLER WILL LEARN:
Language skills

The bear went over the mountain

◆ You will need a stool or bench to serve as the "mountain" for this game. Choose one that your toddler can reach over while standing.

◆ Sit on one side of the stool with your toddler and his teddy bear.

◆ On the other side of the stool, place one of your child's toys, like a ball.

◆ Start singing "The bear went over the mountain" to the tune of "For he's a jolly good fellow". While you sing, make the teddy bear climb the bench and descend the other side.

> *Oh, the bear went over the mountain,*
> *The bear went over the mountain,*
> *The bear went over the mountain*
> *To see what he could see.*

◆ Ask, "What did you see, Teddy Bear? Oh, you saw a ball!"

◆ Play the game again, placing another toy on the other side of the mountain. Your toddler will be anxious to tell what the bear saw on the other side.

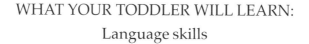

WHAT YOUR TODDLER WILL LEARN:
Language skills

Drop the bear

◆ Play this game while your child is in her cot.

◆ Give her a teddy bear and show her how to drop it from her cot. This shouldn't be too difficult since children this age enjoy dropping things.

◆ Place a large basket next to the cot.

◆ Show your child how to drop the bear into the basket and say, "One, two, drop the bear."

◆ Encourage your toddler to drop the bear into the basket. This game requires skill of your toddler, and she will get much satisfaction from succeeding.

WHAT YOUR TODDLER WILL LEARN:
Hand–eye coordination

The touching game

◆ Playing a touch-and-name game will help your toddler learn more about herself.

◆ Recite this rhyme with your child:

Can you touch your head,
Can you touch your head,
One, two, three,
Can you touch your head?

◆ Repeat the rhyme, naming a different part of the body each time.

◆ After you feel sure that your toddler knows at least three or four parts well, give her a teddy bear and ask her to touch the same parts on the bear.

◆ If she can play this game with the bear, it means that she has understood and acquired the concepts.

WHAT YOUR TODDLER WILL LEARN:
Body awareness

Pretending

◆ Bring teddy along to learn new tasks with your toddler.

◆ Talk to the teddy bear and to your child, for example, "Paul, would you like to drink from the cup?; Teddy, would you like to drink from the cup?" Pretend to give teddy a drink.

◆ There are many things that you can do with teddy and your child together:

- Rock teddy in your arms.
- Give teddy a kiss.
- Hold teddy high in the air.
- Tickle teddy on the tummy.
- Ask teddy to wave "bye-bye".

WHAT YOUR TODDLER WILL LEARN:
Play skills

Teddy bear train

◆ Find several boxes large enough to hold a teddy bear or another stuffed animal.

◆ Hook the boxes together with strong tape or rope.

◆ Ask the teddy bear if he would like to go for a train ride.

◆ Ask your toddler to put the teddy into a box.

◆ Ask your toddler if he wants any of the other animals to go for a ride.

◆ Give the rope to your toddler and see if he can pull the train as you recite this poem:

> *Teddy bear train,*
> *Choo, choo, choo.*
> *Teddy bear train,*
> *Choo, choo, choo,*
> *Go a little faster.*
> *   (talk and pull faster)*
> *Go a little slower.*
> *   (talk and pull slowly)*
> *Everybody at the station.*
> *   (talk very slowly)*
> *STOP!!*

WHAT YOUR TODDLER WILL LEARN:
Coordination

Teddy bear sandwiches

◆ Invite your toddler and teddy to lunch.

◆ With your toddler's help, cut heart shapes out of wholemeal bread with a heart-shaped biscuit cutter.

◆ Cut off the point of the heart, and the bread will look like a teddy bear face.

◆ Spread the teddy bear with peanut butter. NOTE: use cream cheese or another type of spread if your child has a nut allergy.

◆ Make a face with raisins and other nutritious foods.

WHAT YOUR TODDLER WILL LEARN:
Coordination

Listen, teddy

◆ Tell your toddler that you are going to play a game with teddy. Everything that you say, teddy will have to do.

◆ Recite this rhyme:

> *Teddy put your hands up, hands up high.*
> *Teddy put your hands down to your side.*
> *Teddy turn around,*
> *Teddy touch the ground,*
> *Teddy pat your tummy,*
> *One, two, three.*

◆ As you recite, act out the rhyme and ask your child to make teddy do so, too.

WHAT YOUR TODDLER WILL LEARN:

Listening skills

Climbing up the tower

◆ Play this game with your toddler, then show her how to play it with a teddy bear.

◆ Sit your toddler in your lap, holding one of her arms high in the air. As you recite this poem, walk the fingers of your other hand up her arm.

> *I am climbing up the tower,*
> *I am going to ring the bell,*
> *Ding, ding, ding, ding.*

◆ When you say "ding", gently pull her hand as if you were ringing a bell.

◆ Ring the bell different ways. Swing her hand back and forth or pull one finger instead of her whole hand. Open and close her fingers.

◆ Repeat the game with a teddy bear or stuffed animal. Your toddler will enjoy playing this game with her teddy.

WHAT YOUR TODDLER WILL LEARN:

Fun

Fun with teddy

◆ Give your toddler her favourite teddy bear or stuffed animal.

◆ Ask your child to sit the teddy on a chair. When she does so correctly, praise her. Ask her to put the teddy in different places—floor, table, bookshelf, etc.

◆ Recite this poem and act out the words:

> *Teddy bear, teddy bear,*
> *Now I'll put you on the chair.*
> *Teddy bear, teddy bear,*
> *Now I'll give you a kiss.*

◆ Repeat the poem, substituting another word for "chair".

WHAT YOUR TODDLER WILL LEARN:

Language skills

Teddy swing

◆ Tie a length of string or ribbon under the arms of a teddy bear or favourite stuffed animal.

◆ Tie the other end of the string or ribbon to a tree limb to suspend the bear about 60 cm off the ground.

◆ Show your toddler how to push the teddy gently to make it swing.

◆ While enjoying this game very much, children also begin to understand that their push causes the teddy to move.

◆ A nice poem to recite while your child pushes his teddy bear is "The swing" by Robert Louis Stevenson.

WHAT YOUR TODDLER WILL LEARN:
About cause and effect

High and low

◆ Give your toddler his teddy bear and tell him to hold it high in the air.

◆ Tell him to put it down low to the ground.

◆ Sing "Rock a my soul" while you dance around the room. Tell your toddler to hold his teddy bear close and dance around with you. Tell him to hold the bear high in the air and low to the ground when you sing the words "high" and "low".

> *Rock a my soul in the bosom of Abraham,*
> *Rock a my soul in the bosom of Abraham,*
> *Rock a my soul in the bosom of Abraham,*
> *Oh, rock a my soul.*
>
> *So high you can't get over it,*
> *So low you can't get under it,*
> *So wide you can't get around it,*
> *Oh, rock a my soul.*

◆ If you can get a recording of this song, you will both enjoy singing along while you play the game.

WHAT YOUR TODDLER WILL LEARN:
About high and low

Teddy bear magic

◆ Sing a favourite song with your toddler: "Twinkle, twinkle, little star", "Old MacDonald", etc.

◆ Either get a toy piano or create a make-believe piano. Ask your toddler if teddy can play the piano.

◆ Sit teddy at the piano and move his arms over the keys.

◆ Ask your toddler, "What song would you like teddy to play?" Then say to the teddy bear, "Teddy, would you please play [name of song]."

◆ Move teddy bear's arms over the keys again.

◆ Soon you will see your toddler playing this game by himself with his teddy bear.

WHAT YOUR TODDLER WILL LEARN:
Play skills

'Round and 'round and boom

◆ Play the game "Ring-a-ring o'roses" with your toddler.

◆ Say to your child, "Let's play this game with your teddy bear."

◆ Show your child how to dance the teddy bear around in a circle and then fall down with him.

◆ Give the bear to your child and see whether he can play while you sing.

◆ Arrange several stuffed animals in a circle. Play the game with one animal at a time.

WHAT YOUR TODDLER WILL LEARN:

Play skills

Teddy bear, teddy bear

◆ Recite this poem with your toddler and act out the lines:

Teddy bear, teddy bear, turn around.
Teddy bear, teddy bear, touch the ground.
Teddy bear, teddy bear, read the news.
Teddy bear, teddy bear, touch your shoes.
Teddy bear, teddy bear, go upstairs.
Teddy bear, teddy bear, say your prayers.
Teddy bear, teddy bear, turn out the light.
Teddy bear, teddy bear, say "goodnight!"

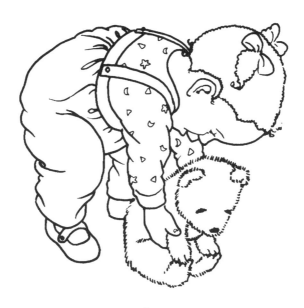

WHAT YOUR TODDLER WILL LEARN:
To follow directions

Where's the teddy?

- ◆ You will need two teddy bears or stuffed animals and two open boxes.

- ◆ Sit on the floor with your toddler and show him different places to put the teddy bear.

- ◆ Each time you tell him where to put the teddy bear, do the movement with him.

- ◆ Sing to the tune of "London Bridge is falling down":

    Put your teddy in the box,
    In the box, in the box.
    Put your teddy in the box,
    Hip, hip, hooray.

    Put your teddy under the box,
    Under the box, under the box.
    Put your teddy under the box,
    Hip, hip, hooray.

- ◆ Try many variations of this song:

    Hold your teddy over the box...
    Put your teddy at the side of the box...
    Put your teddy behind the box...
    Put your teddy in front of the box...
    Sit your teddy in the box...
    Lay your teddy in the box...

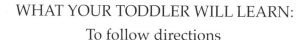

WHAT YOUR TODDLER WILL LEARN:
To follow directions

Lunch with teddy

◆ Tell your toddler that teddy bear will join you for lunch today.

◆ While you set a place at the table for teddy, talk about the things that you are doing: "Here is teddy's dish, teddy's cup," etc.

◆ Encourage your toddler to ask teddy questions: "Will you ask teddy if he likes orange juice?" This will help your child learn what to say. After your child has asked the questions, ask him, "What did teddy say?"

WHAT YOUR TODDLER WILL LEARN:
Socialization skills

Driving teddy

◆ Ask your toddler to "drive the car". Show him how to move his arms from left to right as he turns the make-believe steering wheel.

◆ Walk around the room pretending that you are driving the car.

◆ Once your toddler can do this, ask him to let his teddy bear drive the car.

◆ Show him how to move the teddy's arms.

◆ As you walk around the room driving the car, make car sounds, pretend to beep the horn and put your foot on the brake when you stop.

WHAT YOUR TODDLER WILL LEARN:

Play skills

Three bears

◆ Compose a simple story about three bears. The traditional story is too long and complicated for a toddler.

◆ Here is a possible story:

Once upon a time there were three bears: one (hold up one finger), two (hold up two), three (hold up three). They came to Mary's house (substitute your child's name) to ask Teddy to come and play. Mary and Teddy invited them in for milk and biscuits and play with blocks.

◆ After telling the story, set out three cups and three biscuits.

◆ Repeat the story, and this time, act it out. If you do not have three teddy bears, use any stuffed animal or even a toy.

◆ Invite the bears in for milk and biscuits. Pretend that they are drinking the milk and eating the biscuits.

◆ Get out the blocks and pretend that everyone is playing with them.

WHAT YOUR TODDLER WILL LEARN:
Listening skills

'Round and 'round and stop

◆ Play this game with your child, then add the teddy bear.

◆ Face your toddler and hold his hands. Walk around slowly in a circle, reciting this poem:

> *'Round and around and around we go,*
> *'Round and around and around we go,*
> *'Round and around and around we go,*
> *'Round and around and STOP.*

◆ On the word "STOP", do not move a muscle! Toddlers adore this game and will want to play it again and again.

◆ The next time, walk around in the opposite direction, a little faster.

◆ Repeat this game until you are going pretty fast.

◆ Next, give your child his teddy bear. See if he can play the game with the bear. You may have to demonstrate for him.

WHAT YOUR TODDLER WILL LEARN:
Listening skills

Five little teddy bears

◆ Recite this poem, holding up one finger as you begin. Each time another bear comes along, hold up another finger.

> *One little teddy bear eating some stew,*
> *Along came another bear and then there were two.*
> *Two little teddy bears bouncing on their knees,*
> *Along came another bear and then there were three.*
> *Three little teddy bears knocking at the door,*
> *Along came another bear and then there were four.*
> *Four little teddy bears found a beehive,*
> *Along came another bear and then there were five.*
> *Buzz, buzz, buzz, buzz,*
> *Run away teddy bears.*

◆ On the last line, conceal your hand behind your back.

WHAT YOUR TODDLER WILL LEARN:
Counting

Jumpin' teddy bear

◆ Spread a large towel on the floor.

◆ Place your child's teddy bear in the middle of the towel. Tell your child that the teddy bear is going to jump.

◆ Ask your toddler to hold one end of the towel while you hold the other, saying, "One, two, wheee!" Lift the towel into the air.

◆ Practise so that your toddler will understand whenever she hears "wheee!" to lift up the towel.

◆ The idea is to keep the teddy bear on the towel.

◆ After a few times, move the towel faster in order to toss the teddy bear higher in the air.

◆ Tossing and trying to catch the bear in the towel takes a lot of hand–eye coordination.

WHAT YOUR TODDLER WILL LEARN:
Hand–eye coordination

Teddy on the log

◆ Teach your toddler to play this game with her teddy bear.

◆ Place a teddy bear or stuffed animal in your lap and one in your toddler's.

◆ Bounce the teddy up and down on your knees while you say this rhyme:

> *A teddy sat on a log,*
> *Crying for his mummy.*
> *His eyes were red,*
> *His tears he shed,*
> *And he fell right into the water.*

◆ On the phrase "fell right into the water," open your legs, release the stuffed toy and let it fall to the floor.

◆ Be prepared! Your toddler will want to do this for hours on end.

WHAT YOUR TODDLER WILL LEARN:
Language skills

Spinning teddy

◆ Get two teddy bears or stuffed animals for you and your toddler to hold.

◆ Hold one teddy close to your body and spin around while saying, "Wheee!"

◆ Ask your child to spin around, holding her teddy bear.

◆ Recite this rhyme and act out the lines, holding your teddy bear, and urge your child to do the same:

> *I'm a spinning top, I'm a spinning top.*
> *I can spin, spin, spin until I stop.*
> *I can spin very slow,*
> *I can spin very fast,*
> *I can fall to the ground and BOOM!*

WHAT YOUR TODDLER WILL LEARN:

Fun

Kitchen Games

The tearing game

◆ Toddlers really enjoy tearing things. This is a good game to play in the kitchen where you can supervise your toddler closely.

◆ Collect old magazines, tissue paper, wrapping paper and foil. Each provides an interesting tearing experience because the textures and sounds differ.

◆ Show your child how to tear the paper and drop it into a box. Since toddlers do like to put things in their mouths, keep a close watch.

◆ Wad a piece of paper into a ball and throw it. Show your child how to do this. If she cannot make the ball, do it for her and give it to her to throw.

WHAT YOUR TODDLER WILL LEARN:
Coordination

Pulling strings

◆ While your toddler is in the high chair, he enjoys playing with toys. He also enjoys throwing things on the floor.

◆ Tie string to a few of your child's toys. Tie the other end of the string under his chair. The string allows your child to play with a toy without it falling to the floor. NOTE: Be sure the string is not long enough to pose a choking hazard.

◆ Your toddler will also find it a challenge to pull the strings to retrieve the toys.

WHAT YOUR TODDLER WILL LEARN:
Problem-solving skills

Cereal fun

◆ Seat your toddler in his high chair.

◆ Drop a small piece of dry cereal into a small-mouthed bottle.

◆ Your toddler must figure out that he cannot reach inside to get the cereal and will have to tip the bottle.

◆ Once your child figures this out, the next step is for him to put the cereal into the bottle and then remove it.

◆ Let him remove the cereal and put it into your mouth.

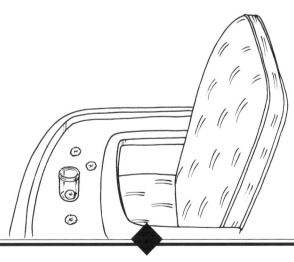

WHAT YOUR TODDLER WILL LEARN:
Problem-solving skills

Fun with rice

♦ Exploring the texture of rice is a wonderful activity for toddlers. It helps them become aware of how something feels, smells and tastes.

♦ Cook and cool some rice.

♦ Put the rice in a large plastic bowl.

♦ Give your child cups and spoons to use to play with the rice.

♦ Show her how to fill up the cups, pick up the rice, separate the grains of rice—a great activity to improve her coordination—and taste the rice.

WHAT YOUR TODDLER WILL LEARN:
About textures

What's in the drawer?

◆ Curiosity is the backbone of a child's development of competence. From your baby's earliest perceptions onwards, he will want to feel and explore everything and experience the world through all of his senses.

◆ In a small, easily opened drawer in the kitchen, place many different objects, like plastic containers, pans, wooden spoons.

◆ Place anything in the drawer that has no sharp edges and is safe for your baby to play with.

◆ Leave the drawer ajar while you are in the kitchen, and you will have a happy, curious companion bent on exploring his drawer.

◆ From time to time, change the contents of the drawer.

WHAT YOUR TODDLER WILL LEARN:
Exploration skills

Paper bag blocks

◆ You will need several large paper grocery bags and lots of newspaper.

◆ Ask your toddler to help you crumple the newspaper and stuff it into the paper bags.

◆ When all the bags are full, close them tightly with tape or string.

◆ These bags have become lightweight blocks that are easy for your toddler to move around.

◆ Experiment with your child and show him different things to do with the paper bag blocks:

  • Stack the blocks.
  • Lay them side by side.
  • Put them in a circle.
  • Throw one back and forth.

◆ Try drawing faces on the bags to turn them into puppets.

WHAT YOUR TODDLER WILL LEARN:
Creativity

Spin around

◆ You will need a kitchen cabinet turntable for this game.

◆ Young children love to spin these turntables and are happy just watching them spin.

◆ Place a small object on the turntable and spin it around. Observe what happens to it.

◆ Tape a small toy to the turntable. Tell your child that you are going to give it a ride.

◆ Each time you spin the turntable, say:

> 'Round and 'round and 'round she goes,
> Where she stops, nobody knows.

◆ Each time the turntable stops, shout, "Hurrah!"

WHAT YOUR TODDLER WILL LEARN:
Language skills

The in and out game

◆ Get a box with individual compartments. When buying things by the case, you often get this kind of box.

◆ Save paper towel tubes or plastic bottles.

◆ Give your child the tubes or bottles to put into the compartments, then remove.

◆ Toddlers will do this happily for long periods.

◆ Ask her to put the tube "in" the box and take it "out".

WHAT YOUR TODDLER WILL LEARN:
Hand–eye coordination

Doll play

◆ This is a wonderful game to play while waiting for a meal.

◆ Give your child his favourite doll or stuffed animal. Ask him about his doll: "Is your [name of doll] hungry? Is he sleepy?"

◆ Direct your child to do things with his doll:

- Give your doll a kiss.
- Hug your baby.
- Rock your baby.
- Give your doll some milk.
- Can you give your baby a bath?
- Change your baby's nappy.

◆ All these directions will elicit some response from your toddler. As he begins to enjoy the directions, his listening skills will become more acute.

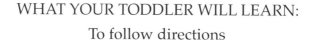

WHAT YOUR TODDLER WILL LEARN:
To follow directions

Where are you?

◆ Play this game while your child is sitting in her high chair.

◆ Pretend that you cannot find your toddler even though she is in plain view. Ask, "Where is [child's name]?"

◆ As you ask, look in different parts of the kitchen. Look in your pocket, a drawer, under the table, behind the high chair, etc.

◆ After you have looked for about a minute, recognize your toddler and act surprised. "There you are!"

◆ This is the time for a big hug and kiss.

WHAT YOUR TODDLER WILL LEARN:
Language skills

Sweeping floors

◆ Helping your toddler imitate what he sees in his environment prepares him for more serious play at an older age.

◆ Find pictures of tasks that you do in the kitchen: washing dishes, eating, sweeping, cooking, and so on.

◆ Show the pictures to your child and talk about each one.

◆ Pick one of the pictures and ask your child about it. If his language is limited, ask questions that he can answer in one word, for example, "Is this Mummy sweeping the floor?"

◆ After you have talked, do the task pictured. "Now Mummy will sweep the floor." Ask your toddler to help.

WHAT YOUR TODDLER WILL LEARN:

Imitation

Three little ducks

Toddlers love this fingerplay

◆ Act out the story with your hand.

> *Three little ducks went out to play,*
> *(hold up three fingers)*
> *Under a bridge and far away.*
> *(wiggle your fingers as if they were swimming)*
> *And the Mummy duck said, "Quack, quack, quack."*
> *(form a duck bill with your hand)*
> *Two little ducks came swimming back.*
> *(hold up two fingers)*
>
> *Two little ducks went out to play,*
> *(hold up two fingers)*
> *Under a bridge and far away.*
> *(wiggle your fingers as if they were swimming)*
> *And the Daddy duck said, "Quack, quack, quack."*
> *(form a duck bill with your hand)*
> *One little duck came swimming back.*
> *(hold up one finger)*
>
> *One little duck went out to play,*
> *(hold up one finger)*
> *Under a bridge and far away.*
> *(wiggle your finger as if it were swimming)*
> *Mummy and Daddy said, "Where are the ducks?"*
> *(form a duck bill with your hand)*
> *"We miss them."*
> *(say this line sadly)*
> *And three little ducks came swimming back.*
> *(wiggle three fingers)*

◆ Repeat, encouraging your toddler to imitate your hand
actions.

WHAT YOUR TODDLER WILL LEARN:
Imitation

Pasta fun

◆ Play games with dried pasta to develop coordination and just to have fun.

◆ You can glue pasta, string it, colour it, paint it and even eat it (after it's cooked).

◆ Pasta comes in many shapes and sizes for sorting, counting and learning colours.

◆ Start your toddler off by stringing large pasta shapes on to shoestrings. As her hand–eye coordination improves, you can string smaller pasta shapes.

◆ Colour small pasta shapes with food colouring and water. Make these treasures into bracelets and necklaces.

◆ Paint large pasta shapes with watercolours.

WHAT YOUR TODDLER WILL LEARN:
About shapes

Sniffing game

◆ Call attention to smells in the air. This is particularly easy when something is baking in the oven.

◆ Seat your baby in his high chair and bring foods for him to sniff.

◆ Show a lemon to your child and say, "This is a lemon." Sniff it and say, "Mmm, it smells good."

◆ Hold the lemon under your baby's nose and ask him to smell it.

WHAT YOUR TODDLER WILL LEARN:
About smells

Squash

◆ This is a floor game to play with toddlers.

◆ Lie on your back, knees bent.

◆ Sit your child on your knees, with her feet in your lap. Hold her hands for security and say, "I'm going to the supermarket and I'm going to buy some bread, cereal, bananas, milk." Name all the food that you can think of.

◆ At the end of your grocery list, loudly say, "SQUASH." Simultaneously straighten your legs so that she bounces downwards.

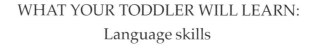

WHAT YOUR TODDLER WILL LEARN:
Language skills

Kitchen band

◆ Get out pots, pans, plastic bowls, wooden spoons, metal spoons and anything else that might make music.

◆ Sit on the floor with your toddler and start banging spoons on to pots. Hit the pots together, the spoons together, etc.

◆ Give a spoon and a pot to your child and encourage her to copy you.

◆ Sing to the tune of "Mary had a little lamb":

> *Pots and pans are fun to play,*
> *Fun to play, fun to play.*
> *Pots and pans are fun to play,*
> *Let's play music.*

WHAT YOUR TODDLER WILL LEARN:
Fun

Matching game

◆ Give your toddler three identical objects, like teaspoons.

◆ Pick up each spoon, name it and pretend that you are eating something.

◆ Let your child hold each spoon, feeling its shape and texture.

◆ Replace one spoon with a fork. Ask him to give you the spoon. Ask for another spoon.

◆ Pick up the fork and say its name. Pretend to eat with it. Let your child hold the fork and feel its shape and texture.

◆ Put out two spoons and a fork. Ask your child to give you the fork. Praise him when he selects the right one.

WHAT YOUR TODDLER WILL LEARN:
About same and different

Tongs game

◆ Gather a group of small toys into a large box or bowl.

◆ Give your toddler a pair of kitchen tongs and show him how to pick up the objects with the tongs.

◆ Once your child easily picks up a toy with the tongs, show him how to move the toy into a different box.

◆ Place a muffin tin next to the box. Show him how to put a toy into a muffin cup, using the tongs. This takes a great deal of coordination.

◆ If you want to make the game harder, try putting the toy into an ice cube tray.

◆ Games like this are a prerequisite for counting.

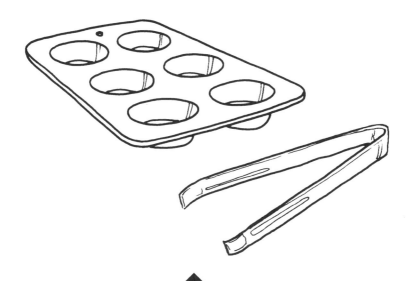

WHAT YOUR TODDLER WILL LEARN:
Coordination

Playdough experiments

◆ The kitchen is a great place to experiment with playdough.

◆ Show your child how to roll a piece of playdough and squeeze it, pound it, poke it and pull it apart.

◆ Give your child some tools to use with the playdough, like an ice lolly stick for poking, cutting, scraping and scooping. She can roll a rolling pin with both hands to flatten the dough.

◆ With biscuit cutters, your child can make pretend biscuits for teddy bears.

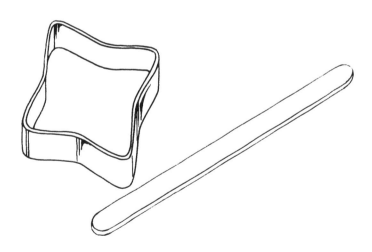

WHAT YOUR TODDLER WILL LEARN:

Creativity

Food talk

◆ The kitchen is a wonderful place to improve your toddler's language skills.

◆ Whenever a child names something that he likes very much, his vocabulary increases.

◆ Place three foods that your child enjoys on his high chair tray.

◆ Touch each one and name it.

◆ Repeat the name and ask your toddler to touch it.

◆ Make up a song about these foods to the tune of "Frère Jacques"

> *Raisins yummy,*
> *Biscuits yummy,*
> *Orange juice too, orange juice too.*
> *Yummy, yummy, yummy,*
> *Down into my tummy,*
> *Good for you, good for you.*

◆ Sing this song about any three foods of your choosing.

WHAT YOUR TODDLER WILL LEARN:
Language skills

Spaghetti game

◆ Cooked spaghetti is a lot of fun for toddlers.

◆ She can squeeze it and feel it slip from her fingers.

◆ She can wiggle it and pretend it is a worm or snake.

◆ She can hold the ends with her hands and try to pull it apart.

◆ Repeat the name and ask your toddler to touch it.

◆ Sing this song (to the tune of "On top of Old Smokey") and mime the actions:

> *On top of spaghetti, all covered with cheese,*
> *(put some grated cheese on top of the spaghetti)*
> *I lost my poor meatball,*
> *(pretend to cry)*
> *When somebody sneezed.*
> *(say "Aachoo!")*

◆ Your toddler will want to play this game over and over. She will also want to eat the spaghetti.

WHAT YOUR TODDLER WILL LEARN:
Language skills

Two little hot dogs

◆ Recite the poem, acting out the story with your toddler.

Two little hot dogs frying in a pan,
The grease got hot, and one went BAM!
One little hot dog frying in the pan,
One went POP! And one went BAM!

No little hot dogs frying in the pan,
The grease got hot, and the pan went BAM!

◆ On the first line of the first and second verses, lie flat on your back on the floor like a hot dog. On the last line of all three verses, wiggle around on the floor.

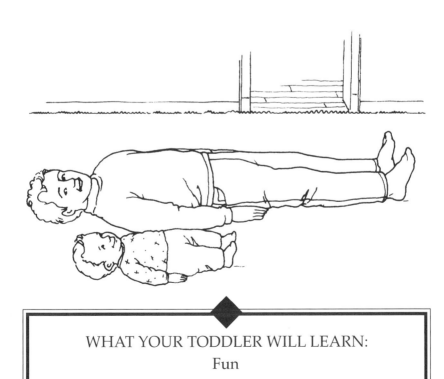

WHAT YOUR TODDLER WILL LEARN:
Fun

Hard and soft

◆ You will need several margarine containers and several small objects, some hard, some soft.

◆ Pencils, ice lolly sticks, small blocks and keys make good hard objects for this game.

◆ Cotton wool balls, scraps of soft material, pieces of sponge, powder puffs and feathers are good soft objects.

◆ Put one object into each container. Give your toddler a container to open and encourage him to remove the object. Talk to him about how the object feels hard or soft and name it. Let him feel and explore it.

◆ Continue giving him containers with soft objects. Each time, let him remove the lid and feel what is inside.

◆ When you have finished the soft objects, repeat with the hard objects.

WHAT YOUR TODDLER WILL LEARN:
About hard and soft

Five green peas

◆ Sit your toddler in her high chair. Place some peas in front of her.

◆ Pick up a pea and put it into your mouth, saying, "Oh, these are so delicious."

◆ Ask your toddler to pick up a pea. After she puts it in her mouth, say, "Isn't that good?" Talk about the peas, their colour, their shape, etc.

◆ After your toddler has finished eating, take her out of the high chair, recite this poem and imitate the peas with her as suggested:

> *Five tiny green peas,*
> *Lying in a row,*
> > *(lie down on the floor)*
> *Inside a small green pod,*
> *One day began to grow.*
> *They grew and they grew,*
> > *(start getting up from the floor)*
> *And they didn't stop,*
> > *(keep getting up)*
> *Until one day, their pod went POP!*
> > *(jump up in the air)*

WHAT YOUR TODDLER WILL LEARN:
Imaginative play

Baster game

◆ This game is a challenge, and your toddler will love it, squeezing and watching the liquid.

◆ Arrange two medium-sized plastic bowls next to one another.

◆ Fill one bowl with water. Add food colouring to the water for artistic purposes.

◆ Show your toddler how to put the baster into the water and squeeze the bulb. Show her where to look to see the water filling up the tube.

◆ Show her how to empty the baster into the second bowl.

WHAT YOUR TODDLER WILL LEARN:
Coordination

Outside Games

Grass exercise

◆ Take off your shoes and run around in the grass with your toddler.

◆ Stretch your arms high in the air, then low to the ground.

◆ After a few stretches, recite this poem with your child and see whether she will copy you:

> *Up to the sky,*
> *Down to the grass.*
> *Up to the sky,*
> *Down to the grass.*
> *Turn around,*
> *Now fall down.*

◆ Stretch your arms up and down as the poem directs, then turn in a circle on the fifth line.

◆ On the last line, fall down and say, "BOOM!"

WHAT YOUR TODDLER WILL LEARN:
Coordination

Happy feet

◆ Walking on a variety of surfaces helps young children develop good eye–foot coordination.

◆ Walk barefoot on smooth pebbles. Talk about how your feet feel. Walk barefoot in sand. Notice that you have to carry your body differently on pebbles than on sand.

◆ Barefoot, try walking on pillows, logs, grass, cement, bricks and other surfaces.

◆ Each time that you vary the surface, you adjust your body, which develops eye–foot coordination.

WHAT YOUR TODDLER WILL LEARN:
Coordination

Washing stones

◆ Place several stones of different shapes and sizes into a plastic bucket.

◆ Go outside with your child, bringing with you the bucket of stones, old rags and a jug of water.

◆ Fill the bucket with water and wash the stones with a rag. Give your toddler a rag and encourage him to copy you.

◆ As you wash, sing to the tune of "Here we go 'round the mulberry bush":

> *This is the way we wash the stones,*
> *Wash the stones, wash the stones.*
> *This is the way we wash the stones,*
> *So early in the morning.*

◆ Observe that many stones change their colour and texture when washed.

WHAT YOUR TODDLER WILL LEARN:
About textures

Ball game

◆ Take two balls of the same size outside. One ball is for you and one for your toddler.

◆ Show your toddler all the different things that you can do with the ball by singing about it to the tune of "Here we go 'round the mulberry bush".

> *This is the way we roll the ball,*
> *Roll the ball, roll the ball.*
> *This is the way we roll the ball,*
> *Every single day.*
>
> *This is the way we hold the ball…*
> *(hold the ball above your head, under your arm,*
> *behind your back)*

◆ Give your toddler a ball and let him copy what you do.

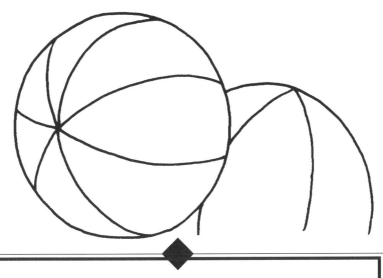

WHAT YOUR TODDLER WILL LEARN:
Language skills

Neighbourhood visit

◆ Toddlers adore this game. It not only develops their language, but helps them become familiar with their surroundings.

◆ Take your toddler for a walk around the neighbourhood. As you pass interesting things, stop and talk to them.

◆ Talk to the flowers, the insects, the grass and so forth, saying something like:

"Hello, grass. My name is Susie. We are taking a walk around the neighbourhood. Bye-bye."

◆ Repeat the sequence each time you decide to talk to something.

WHAT YOUR TODDLER WILL LEARN:
Language skills

Washing fun

◆ Water and young children are definitely attracted to one another.

◆ Fill a bucket or large pan with water.

◆ Give your child a flannel or small sponge, plastic dinnerware, old cutlery and anything else that he can pretend to wash.

◆ While you are outside, there are many other things that he could try to wash, like tables, chairs, etc.

WHAT YOUR TODDLER WILL LEARN:
To follow directions

Outside treasures

◆ There are so many treasures outdoors. Take a basket and go exploring with your toddler.

◆ As you find things, put them into the treasure basket. Stones, seed-pods, twigs, leaves, flowers, pebbles and shells are just a few of the many treasures you will discover.

◆ After you have gathered several treasures, take each one out and talk about it.

◆ Pay close attention to the ones in which your toddler seems particularly interested, since this will give you ideas for future learning experiences.

◆ Ask your toddler for one of the treasures to return to the basket. See if he can remember its name.

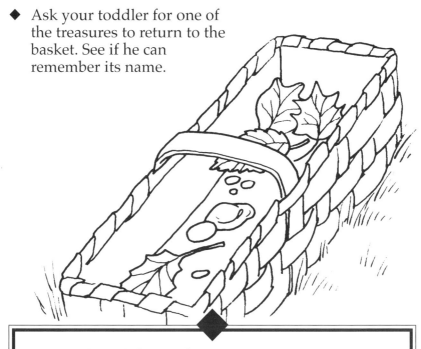

WHAT YOUR TODDLER WILL LEARN:

Nature appreciation

The dandelion game

◆ Take your child for a dandelion walk.

◆ Pick a dandelion to hold. See how many more dandelions you can find along your walk.

◆ Examine the dandelion with your child. Look at it through a magnifying glass.

◆ Use words like "delicately" and "gently" to describe how to hold a dandelion.

◆ Pick a bouquet of dandelions to put in a vase at home.

◆ Compare the dandelions to other yellow things in your house.

WHAT YOUR TODDLER WILL LEARN:
Nature appreciation

The rolling game

♦ Whenever you do an activity with your toddler, practise it on both right and left sides. Even though toddlers are too young to understand left and right, they can recognize that their bodies have two sides.

♦ Find a gentle grassy slope or mound.

♦ Show your child how to lie on her side and roll down the hill. You may have to push her at first.

♦ Then show your child how to lie on her other side and roll.

♦ Once your toddler can roll by herself, go to the bottom of the slope and catch her.

♦ It's lots of fun to play, "I'm going to catch you," by rolling after her down the hill.

WHAT YOUR TODDLER WILL LEARN:
About left and right

The line game

◆ Lines can be made in sand, soil and mud.

◆ Show your toddler how to make a line in the soil with his finger.

◆ Guide his hand gently to help him make a line. Praise your toddler.

◆ Next, make a wiggly line. Help your toddler do the same.

◆ Try making lines with other objects like a stick or a toy.

◆ Push a toy car through the soil and show your toddler the tyre tracks.

◆ These experiences acquaint your child with lines and develop hand–eye coordination.

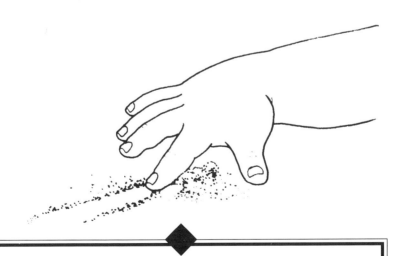

WHAT YOUR TODDLER WILL LEARN:
Coordination

Get the beanbag

◆ This game can be played with one or more people. You will need a basket and some beanbags.

◆ Your task is to toss the beanbags into the basket. Your toddler's task is to take the beanbags out of the basket and give them back to you.

◆ If your toddler is walking, she will more easily remove the beanbags without your help.

◆ If your toddler is not yet walking, tip the basket to help her remove the beanbags.

◆ Soon your little cherub will be trying to throw the beanbags herself.

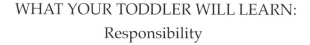

WHAT YOUR TODDLER WILL LEARN:

Responsibility

Tumbling fun

◆ Get down on the floor with your toddler and roll over, asking her, "I am rolling over. Can you roll over?"

◆ Demonstrate different movements and see if she can copy you. Each time, tell her what you are doing and ask whether she can do it.

◆ Toddlers like to roll, squat, run and touch a tree, stand on their heads, spread their arms wide, etc.

◆ Naming the actions as you do them develops language skills.

WHAT YOUR TODDLER WILL LEARN:
To follow directions

Pillow swing

◆ You will need a length of elastic and a lightweight pillow or cushion.

◆ Sew one end of the elastic to the corner of the pillow and tie the other end to a tree branch. The pillow should hang low enough for your toddler to reach it with a swing of her arm.

◆ Hit the pillow with your hand while you say to your child, "One, two, three, BOOM!"

◆ Say it again and encourage your child to copy you.

◆ Give your toddler different things with which to hit the pillow, like paper towel tubes, a fly swatter or a lightweight branch.

WHAT YOUR TODDLER WILL LEARN:
Imitation

Sprinkle time

- ◆ Poke holes in the bottom of a large plastic bottle.

- ◆ Go outside with your toddler and talk about the grass, the flowers and all the things in your garden.

- ◆ Fill the plastic bottle with water from the hose and tell your child where to sprinkle the water.

- ◆ Ask your child to sprinkle the grass, the path, the flowers, etc. Each time your toddler understands your directions, praise her.

- ◆ Sing to the tune of "This old man" as you sprinkle:

> *Sprinkle time, sprinkle time,*
> *Now it's time for sprinkle time.*
> *With a shake, shake, shakey shake,*
> *Water everywhere.*
> *Sprinkle time is here again.*

WHAT YOUR TODDLER WILL LEARN:
Hand–eye coordination

The jungle game

◆ Get down on the floor with your toddler and demonstrate how to squirm like a snake.

◆ Set a chair in the middle of the floor and slither around it with your toddler.

◆ Try making a tunnel to slither through by placing two or three chairs side by side and covering them with a blanket.

◆ Squirm through the tunnel with your toddler. As you squirm along, sing to the tune of "London Bridge is falling down":

In the jungle goes the snake,
Goes the snake, goes the snake.
In the jungle goes the snake,
Squirm, squirm, hiss!

WHAT YOUR TODDLER WILL LEARN:
Body awareness

Fun with streamers

◆ Crepe paper streamers are wonderful toys for toddlers. Here are some ways to play with them outside:

- Run with a streamer in your hand.
- Twirl a streamer around in your hand.
- Hold the streamer low to the ground and encourage your child to jump over it.
- Tie several streamers to a tree branch low enough that your child can jump and hit them.
- On a windy day, simply hold the streamer in the air and watch it ripple in the wind.

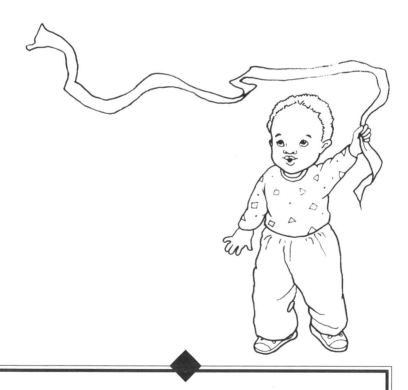

WHAT YOUR TODDLER WILL LEARN:
Coordination

I'm hiding

◆ This is an exciting game greatly enjoyed by toddlers.

◆ At a moment when your toddler is not looking, hide yourself close by and say, "I'm hiding, come and find me."

◆ Hide behind something that leaves you partially visible, such as a bush, a tree or the side of a house.

◆ Your child will learn to listen for the direction of your voice, then use his eyes to find you.

◆ This game also helps your toddler understand that a visible shoulder and arm are attached to a whole body.

◆ Your toddler will be so thrilled to find you. It's a perfect time for a big hug.

WHAT YOUR TODDLER WILL LEARN:
Listening skills

Paint the world

◆ Give your toddler a paintbrush and bucket of water outside.

◆ Sing to the tune of "Here we go 'round the mulberry bush":

> *This is the way we paint the house,*
> *Paint the house, paint the house.*
> *This is the way we paint the house,*
> *Every single day.*

◆ Let your child paint the house with water.

◆ Sing the same song about the pavement, porch, dustbin, car, and whatever else can be "painted" with water.

WHAT YOUR TODDLER WILL LEARN:
Language skills

I'm a walkin'

◆ This is truly a favourite game. Walk with your toddler as you recite this poem, holding her hand:

> *I'm a walkin', walkin', walkin',*
> *I'm a walkin', walkin', walkin',*
> *I'm a walkin', walkin', walkin',*
> *Then I stop.*

◆ Walk in a circle. When you come to the word "stop", freeze in place.

◆ Instead of walking, try hopping, jumping, skating, tiptoeing, marching, running, swimming and turning around.

◆ Your toddler will know exactly what to do on the word "stop", and may even surprise you by saying the word.

WHAT YOUR TODDLER WILL LEARN:
Coordination

Blowing games

◆ Toddlers enjoy blowing. While it requires skill to learn, practice also strengthens the mouth for language development. Here are some ways for your child to blow:

- Blow air through straws.
- Blow bubbles in a large cup of water.
- Blow on your fingers.
- Blow on one finger.
- Blow air into a paper bag.
- Blow a leaf off your hand.
- Blow a small, lightweight ball around the room with a straw.
- Blow a flower or blade of grass.

WHAT YOUR TODDLER WILL LEARN:
Language skills

Dickery dare

◆ Play this game either sitting with your toddler in your lap or standing and holding your child.

◆ Recite this rhyme and bounce your child as directed:

> *Dickery, dickery, dare,*
> *(bounce your toddler)*
> *The pig flew up in the air.*
> *(lift him high in the air)*
> *The man in brown,*
> *(continue bouncing)*
> *Soon brought him down.*
> *(stop bouncing and hold still)*
> *Dickery, dickery, dare.*
> *(start bouncing again)*

WHAT YOUR TODDLER WILL LEARN:

Fun

Pop, goes the baby

◆ Sit in a grassy area with your child facing you.

◆ Bend your knees and touch the soles of your feet together.

◆ Help your toddler do the same thing.

◆ Bend your body forward while holding on to your ankles. Hide your face between your legs.

◆ Sing the song "Pop, goes the weasel". When you sing the word "pop", snap your body up to a sitting position.

◆ If your toddler needs help, hold his body down while you sing and guide him back up on "pop".

WHAT YOUR TODDLER WILL LEARN:
Fun

Tunnel ball

◆ You need three or four people to play this game. Older siblings, friends and neighbours will enjoy playing with you and your toddler.

◆ Ask them to stand in line with their legs apart.

◆ One person should stand at the end of the row to catch the ball.

◆ Show your toddler how to roll the ball through the tunnel of legs to the catcher.

◆ Continue playing until your child can roll the ball unaided.

◆ Let your toddler have a turn being the catcher.

WHAT YOUR TODDLER WILL LEARN:
To roll a ball

Run to the tree

◆ One thing that toddlers love is to run. This game will give your toddler an opportunity to run and improve his language skills.

◆ Walk around the garden with your toddler. Tie colourful ribbon in two or three places—a tree, a door, a familiar area.

◆ Say to your toddler, "I'm going to run to the tree." Holding his hand, run to the tree. Run to the other places, each time telling him where you're going.

◆ Next, ask your toddler to run to the tree, the door, etc. He will adore this, especially if you praise him greatly when he reaches his destination.

WHAT YOUR TODDLER WILL LEARN:
Language skills

Walking games

◆ Once your toddler has learned to walk, there are many activities to increase her coordination.

◆ Show her how to walk different ways: sideways, backwards, or high-legged like a horse.

◆ March, walk on tiptoe or slide your feet.

◆ Hang your arms in front of you, your hands clasped and swaying back and forth. Walk slowly as you swing your "elephant trunk".

◆ Walk slowly and walk fast.

◆ Encourage your child to hop, jump, skip and run.

◆ Walk while talking in different voices: a low voice, a high voice, a baby voice, etc.

WHAT YOUR TODDLER WILL LEARN:
Coordination

Playing catch

◆ A partially deflated beach ball is excellent for a beginner. It should be easy for your child to grasp.

◆ Another adult should stand about one metre from your child to throw the ball.

◆ Stand behind your toddler and guide his hands through the first few catches and tosses.

◆ Show your toddler how to make a cradle with his arms to catch the ball.

◆ Ask the other player to toss the ball.

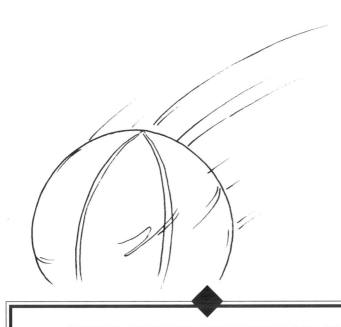

WHAT YOUR TODDLER WILL LEARN:
To play ball

Jumping game

◆ This is a wonderful game that requires strength, balance, coordination and agility.

◆ Find a box strong enough to support your toddler's weight.

◆ Set your toddler on the box and take both of his hands in yours.

◆ "Ready, steady, GO!" Help him jump off the box. Your arms should be at his shoulder height so that he lands on his own weight.

◆ He will love this and want to do it again and again.

WHAT YOUR TODDLER WILL LEARN:

To jump

Magnifying fun

◆ You will need a magnifying glass, preferably plastic.

◆ Go outside with your toddler and sit on a blanket in the grass.

◆ Give a blade of grass to your child. Show him how to look at it through the magnifying glass. Talk about how much bigger it looks.

◆ Help your child examine his body with the magnifying glass. Fingernails, skin—especially something with a plaster on it— and toenails are fascinating.

◆ Walk around the garden and see what you can find. Look at a leaf, and under a leaf. Examine a flower or the bark of a tree.

◆ Get on the ground and see if you can find any crawling things.

◆ Your child will probably want to carry the magnifying glass around all the time.

WHAT YOUR TODDLER WILL LEARN:
Observation skills

Sand play

◆ Making designs in the sand can be wonderfully creative. Your little artist will get much pleasure from playing with sand.

◆ In your kitchen drawers you will find many utensils that make interesting designs in the sand: spatula, slotted spoon, measuring cups, pizza cutter, zester and biscuit cutters, to name a few.

◆ Show your toddler how to put each utensil into the sand to make a design.

◆ If the sand is a little damp, make a mound so the design will show up better.

◆ Show your toddler how to fill a cup with sand, then turn it over to make a hill.

◆ Make a hole in the sand and stick a utensil into it.

◆ Demonstrating these tools to your toddler will inspire her to create her own designs.

◆ Instead of sand, fill a large baking pan with salt and make designs in the salt. To erase, just shake the pan.

WHAT YOUR TODDLER WILL LEARN:
Creativity

Blanket surprise

◆ You will need a small blanket and a ball to play this game.

◆ Hold two corners of the blanket while your toddler holds the other two.

◆ Show her how to shake the blanket.

◆ Put a ball in the centre of the blanket, and see whether you can make it bounce by shaking the blanket.

◆ When the ball drops, let her chase it and put it back into the blanket.

◆ This is a lot of fun. Your toddler will want to put other things into the blanket besides the ball.

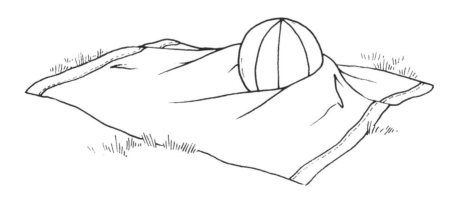

WHAT YOUR TODDLER WILL LEARN:
Hand–eye coordination

Laughing and Having Fun Games

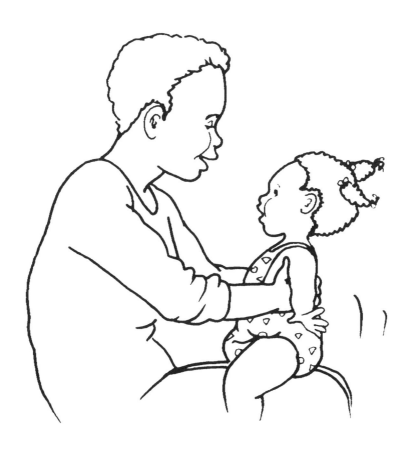

Peek-a-boo

◆ Play "Peek-a-boo" with your child many different ways.

◆ Cover your eyes with your hands.

◆ Place the child's hands over her eyes.

◆ Hang a blanket between you and your child. Peek out at the side, top and bottom of the blanket.

◆ Peek around a large toy, doll, flannel or towel.

◆ Lay your toddler on the bed. Toss a lightweight blanket over her body and lift it up and down as you peek under.

WHAT YOUR TODDLER WILL LEARN:
Bonding

Pat-a-cake

◆ Your child will never tire of this favourite poem.

> *Pat-a-cake, pat-a-cake,*
> *(clap your hands together)*
> *Baker's man,*
> *Bake me a cake as fast as you can.*
> *Roll it and pat it,*
> *And mark it with a "B",*
> *(trace the letter on your hand)*
> *And put it in the oven*
> *(pretend to close the oven door)*
> *For baby and me.*
> *(point to your child, then to yourself)*

◆ First, recite the poem and act out the story. Next, recite the poem and guide your toddler's hands through the motions. Soon your child will imitate you and perform the movements alone.

◆ Instead of the letter "B", say your child's name.

WHAT YOUR TODDLER WILL LEARN:
Language skills

Where's the chick?

◆ Hide behind a door and say, "Cheep, cheep, cheep."

◆ Ask your toddler to find the baby chick.

◆ If she has trouble, stick out your head or foot so that she can see you.

◆ Hide somewhere different and play the game again.

◆ Change the animal to a baby cow or baby duck, etc. Each time make the sounds appropriate to that animal.

◆ After a few times, your child will want to hide and make the animal sounds herself.

WHAT YOUR TODDLER WILL LEARN:

Language skills

The beehive

◆ Show your child pictures of bumble-bees. Make a buzzing sound and see if your toddler can imitate you.

◆ Pretend to be a bumble-bee flying around the room making a buzzing sound.

◆ Recite this rhyme, beginning with your hand clenched into a fist to signify a beehive.

> *This is the beehive,*
> *Where are the bees?*
> *Hidden away where nobody sees.*
> *Watch, and you'll see them come out of the hive,*
> *One, two, three, four, five!*

◆ As you count each bee, bring out a finger, beginning with your thumb.

WHAT YOUR TODDLER WILL LEARN:
Language skills

Can you catch me?

◆ Crawl on the floor with your toddler, saying, "Can you catch me?"

◆ Crawl ahead of your child with excitement so that he pursues you. Be sure to let him catch you.

◆ Switch roles and say, "I'm going to get you!" Let your child crawl ahead.

◆ This is great fun for children, and they will want to play the game over and over.

◆ Whenever you "get" your toddler, give him a big hug.

WHAT YOUR TODDLER WILL LEARN:

Fun

Hot and cold

◆ Sit in a chair with your toddler on your lap facing you.

◆ Say, "I'm so-o-o-o hot," and lift the child up into your arms with a great big hug.

◆ Say, "I'm so-o-o-o cold," and open your legs. Ease the child down to the floor while you hold her firmly.

◆ After a few times, ask the child whether she wants hot or cold. Act out whichever she selects.

◆ After your toddler has learned this game, suggest that she play it with a stuffed animal.

WHAT YOUR TODDLER WILL LEARN:
About opposites

Where am I?

◆ Tell your toddler that you are going to hide.

◆ Hide behind a chair or under a table. The most important thing is that your child sees where you hide so that he can find you.

◆ After you have hidden, sing to the tune of "Frère Jacques":

> *Can you find me, can you find me?*
> *Where am I, where am I?*
> *I am under the table.*
> *I am under the table.*
> *Where am I, where am I?*

◆ When your child comes to get you, give him a big hug.

◆ As you continue this game, go into different rooms in the house.

◆ Your toddler gains confidence in going from room to room and learns more about his house.

WHAT YOUR TODDLER WILL LEARN:
Listening skills

Fun with hats

◆ Put a hat on your head and talk to your toddler in a playfully formal voice: "How do you do, my dear?" or "Oh, so nice to see you."

◆ Put the hat on your toddler's head and repeat the greeting.

◆ Repeat the activity looking into a mirror with your toddler.

◆ Next, wear a different hat. Change your voice and say different words.

◆ Repeat the game until the toddler tires of it.

WHAT YOUR TODDLER WILL LEARN:
Creativity

Looking through the window

♦ Cut two holes in one side of a cardboard box such as a shoe box.

♦ On the opposite side, cut a "window".

♦ Show your toddler how to look through the paired holes.

♦ While he looks through the holes, look through the "window". What fun to see a familiar face!

♦ Stick your finger through the window and wiggle as he watches it.

♦ He will soon learn to watch through the paired holes while putting things through the window from the other side.

WHAT YOUR TODDLER WILL LEARN:

Fun

Blowing bubbles

◆ An inexpensive jar of bubble liquid will provide hours of giggles for you and your toddler.

◆ Blow bubbles outside on both a calm day and a windy day.

◆ Make bubbles by waving the bubble wand in the air rather than blowing through it.

◆ See how many bubbles you can catch on the wand.

◆ See how many bubbles you can count at one time.

◆ Blow bubbles in front of a fan.

◆ Try to catch all the bubbles before they reach the ground.

◆ Step on the bubbles. Where do they go when they pop?

◆ Teach your toddler to blow bubbles. Practice in shaping his mouth to blow will promote language development.

WHAT YOUR TODDLER WILL LEARN:
Fun

Clippety clop

◆ Recite this poem while holding your toddler on your knee:

> Clippety, clippety, clippety clop,
> Over the hills we go.
> Jumping up, jumping down,
> Jumping over the snow.

◆ Bounce your child up and down gently to the words "Clippety, clippety, clippety, clop, over the hills we go."

◆ On the words "Jumping up", lift your toddler high in the air. Ask him to hold his arms over his head.

◆ On the words "jumping down", ease him down.

◆ Resume the bouncing motion on the line "Jumping over the snow."

WHAT YOUR TODDLER WILL LEARN:
Fun

Two bouncing games

◆ Recite this rhyme, bouncing your child on your knees or ankles:

> *Trot, trot to Boston town*
> *To get a stick of candy.*
> *One for me and one for you,*
> *And one for Dicky Dandy.*

◆ On the last line, slide your child gently to one side.

◆ Set your toddler on your knees facing you. Raise one leg at a time, galloping with the rocking horse. Give her a big hug on "whoa!"

> *Rickety, rickety, rocking horse,*
> *Over the fields we go.*
> *Rickety, rickety, rocking horse,*
> *Giddy up, giddy up, whoa!*

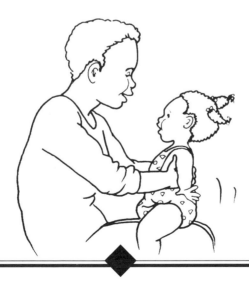

WHAT YOUR TODDLER WILL LEARN:
Fun

Choo, choo

◆ Spread a large beach towel on the floor.

◆ Sit your toddler on the towel. Use the towel to pull her very slowly across the floor.

◆ Pretend with her that she is travelling in something. If it's a car, make a car sound. If it's an aeroplane, make an aeroplane sound. If it's a train, make a "choo, choo" sound.

◆ Even though toddlers may not understand the mode of transport, they enjoy making the sounds.

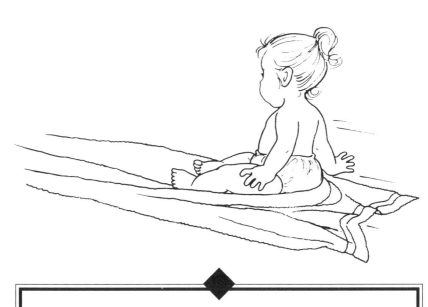

WHAT YOUR TODDLER WILL LEARN:
Balance

Squeaky eakie

◆ Hide a squeeze toy that squeaks under your toddler's pillow or under a couch or chair cushion. Don't let your child see you.

◆ Put your hand under the cushion and squeeze the toy.

◆ If your toddler reacts, listening or searching for the sound, continue squeaking until she uncovers it.

◆ When she finds the toy, say enthusiastically, "Squeaky eakie!"

◆ If your toddler seems confused, show her the toy, then hide it again while she watches.

◆ After she has watched you hide the toy, squeak it again. If she still does not know what to do, guide her hand to the toy and exclaim, "Squeaky eakie!"

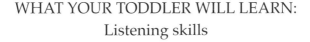

WHAT YOUR TODDLER WILL LEARN:
Listening skills

Puppet fun

◆ With a small hand puppet, you can play many games with your toddler. After you have played, you will find your child playing the games by herself.

◆ Fit the puppet on your hand and talk to your toddler in a disguised voice. Ask her questions about herself: "What's your name; can you wave bye-bye," etc.

◆ Give the puppet to your toddler and suggest ways to play with it: "Can you make the puppet lie down? Can you make the puppet go to sleep? Can you make the puppet jump up and down?"

WHAT YOUR TODDLER WILL LEARN:
Language skills

Puppet pal

◆ Playing with puppets is a wonderful way to develop language in young children.

◆ Stuff a pillowcase full of fabric scraps, anything soft and clean.

◆ Tie it shut with string or rope.

◆ Draw a happy face on the pillowcase puppet.

◆ Show the new friend to your toddler. You might name the puppet something silly like "Orky Morky" or "Diddle Daddle".

◆ Talk to the puppet and pretend that it is talking to you. Ask the puppet questions that your toddler understands: "Do you like to go bye-bye? Did you drink all your milk?"

◆ The more you talk with the puppet and encourage your toddler to do the same, the better language skills your toddler will develop.

WHAT YOUR TODDLER WILL LEARN:
Language skills

Mixie Maxie

◆ Set your toddler on your knees facing you. Recite this poem:

> *Mixie Maxie and the old grey mare*
> *Went off to see the county fair.*
> *The bridge fell down,*
> *The bridge fell in,*
> *So Mixie Maxie went back again.*

◆ On the words "down" and "in", open your legs and let your child fall through; lift him back up immediately. Hold him at the waist for better control.

◆ Show your toddler how toplay this game with a doll or stuffed animal.

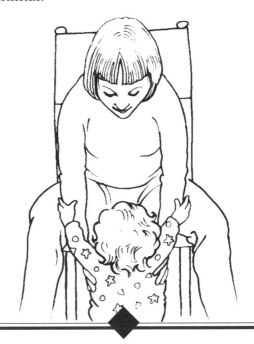

WHAT YOUR TODDLER WILL LEARN:
Bonding

If you're a good boy/girl

◆ This game will excite lots of laughter.

◆ Walk your fingers up your child's leg, starting on the ankle, while you recite this poem:

> *If you're a good boy,*
> *As I'm sure you MUST be,*
> *You won't even laugh,*
> *When I tickle your knee!*

◆ Tickle your child on the knee when you say, "tickle your knee!"

◆ Repeat the poem, changing "knee" to a another part of the body.

◆ Once your child knows this game, recite the poem while he tickles you on your knee.

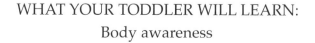

WHAT YOUR TODDLER WILL LEARN:
Body awareness

The exercise game

◆ Hold your toddler's hands as you face each other.

◆ Sing to the tune of "The farmer's in his den" while you jump up and down:

> *Jumping up and down,*
> *We're jumping up and down,*
> *Getting lots of exercise,*
> *We're jumping up and down.*

◆ Vary the words, always keeping the third line the same.

> *Bend and touch our toes,*
> *We bend and touch our toes,*
> *Getting lots of exercise,*
> *We bend and touch our toes.*

◆ Also try "stretching way up high", "running in our place", "twisting side to side".

WHAT YOUR TODDLER WILL LEARN:

Exercise

Little fish

◆ Recite this poem with the palms of your hands pressed together to make a fish.

> *Little fish, little fish,*
> *Goes out to play,*
> *Wiggles his fins and swims away.*
> *He swims and swims in the water bright,*
> *Opens his mouth*
> *And takes a bite.*
> *Mmm, mmm, tastes good!*

◆ Move your hands back and forth like a swimming fish, beginning on the second line. Open and close your hands like a mouth when the fish takes a bite.

◆ On the last line, rub your stomach.

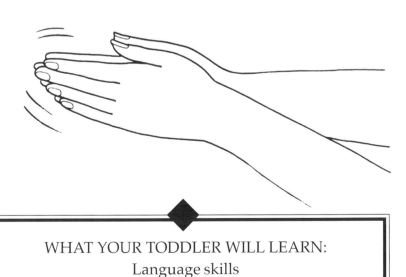

WHAT YOUR TODDLER WILL LEARN:
Language skills

A torch game

◆ Toddlers love this game, which is wonderful for learning language.

◆ Darken a room and sit on the floor with your toddler in your lap.

◆ Move a torch slowly around the room. As you do, talk about what the torch shines upon.

◆ Give the torch to your toddler and encourage her to move the light around the room.

◆ After you have talked about the many things in the room—door, floor, ceiling, doorknob, picture, chair— play another game. Say, "One, two, three, ta dah!"

◆ On the words "ta dah", flash the light somewhere and name the object upon which the light shines.

WHAT YOUR TODDLER WILL LEARN:
Language skills

Looking for a rainbow

◆ There are many ways to play with a garden hose:

- Spray the water in a high arc, and let your toddler run under the water.
- Shoot the water in a stream a few inches off the ground so your child can jump over.
- Raise the stream and encourage your toddler to crawl under.
- Wiggle the water back and forth like a snake.
- Let your toddler water the flowers and grass.
- Make a mud or sand puddle.
- Hang the hose over a tree limb or swing frame, and let the water run in a steady stream.
- Look for a rainbow while you spray the water overhead.

◆ Join in the fun. Let your toddler spray you, too!

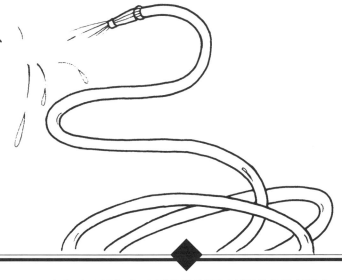

WHAT YOUR TODDLER WILL LEARN:
Observation skills

The sand game

◆ A sandpit or sand table is a wonderful toy for young children.

◆ Many skills can be developed while playing in sand.

◆ Here are activities to do with sand:

• Fill and empty cups and containers.
• Make roads and drive cars over them.
• Bury your bare feet in the sand.
• Bury toys and find them.

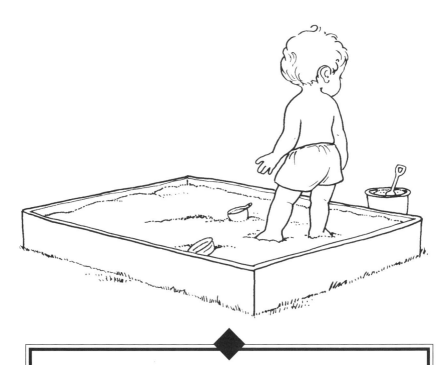

WHAT YOUR TODDLER WILL LEARN:
Imaginative play

Crisscross, apple sauce

◆ Recite this poem with your child.

> *Crisscross,*
> *(draw an X on his back)*
> *Apple sauce,*
> *(tap his nose to the rhythm of the words)*
> *Spiders climbing up your back.*
> *(tickle his back)*
> *Cool breeze,*
> *(blow gently on the back of his neck)*
> *Tight squeeze,*
> *(give him a hug)*
> *And now you've got the shivers.*
> *(tickle him all over)*

WHAT YOUR TODDLER WILL LEARN:
Bonding

One little elephant

◆ Enjoy this silly poem with your toddler:

> *One little elephant went out to play,*
>   *(make an elephant trunk with your arm held in*
>   *front of your face)*
> *Out on a spider's web one day.*
>   *(pretend to walk carefully on a spider's web)*
> *He had such enormous fun,*
> *That he called for another elephant to come.*
>   *(motion for another elephant—your toddler)*
> *Too many elephants … CRASH!*
>   *(fall down with your toddler)*

◆ Another variation teaches colours:

> *One little elephant went out to play,*
> *Out on the busy street one day.*
> *He had such enormous fun,*
> *That he called for a yellow car to come.*
> *Too many cars … CRASH!*

◆ Use toy cars and vary the colours of the cars.

◆ Also try saying, "He had such enormous fun that he called for a yellow car to come, a red car to come, a blue car to come." Get all of the cars together before you say "Too many cars … CRASH!"

WHAT YOUR TODDLER WILL LEARN:

Fun

Abracadabra

◆ On large sheets of paper, trace around objects familiar to your child-blocks, cutlery, a favourite toy, biscuit cutters.

◆ Put these objects into a box.

◆ Recite this poem with your child:

> *Abracadabra, one, two, three,*
> *Look in the box, what do I see?*

◆ Ask your toddler to pick an object from the box. Help her match it to the outline that you drew.

◆ The poem makes this game very special. Closing your eyes while you recite makes it even more fun.

WHAT YOUR TODDLER WILL LEARN:
Observation skills

Picking up the toys

◆ Singing is a gentle and pleasant way to accompany a necessary task.

◆ When your toddler begins to tire of toys with which she has been playing, invite her to help you pick them up.

◆ Sit beside her and demonstrate how to pick up a container and drop a toy into it.

◆ Hand her a toy and ask her to put it into the container.

◆ Hand another toy to her and ask her to drop it into the container.

◆ As you continue dropping toys into the container, sing to the tune of "The farmer's in his den".

> *We're picking up the toys,*
> *We're picking up the toys,*
> *High ho the derry-o,*
> *We're picking up the toys.*

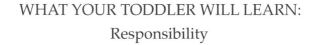

WHAT YOUR TODDLER WILL LEARN:
Responsibility

Grandma's glasses

◆ Recite this poem with your toddler and act out the words with your hands:

> Here are Grandma's glasses,
>   (make circles with your thumb and index finger)
> And here is Grandma's hat.
>   (join your thumbs and index fingertips in a
>   triangle and place on your head)
> Here's the way she folds her hands,
>   (fold your hands)
> And puts them in her lap.
>   (place your hands in your lap)
> Here are Grandpa's glasses,
>   (make bigger glasses with your fingers)
> And here is Grandpa's hat.
>   (make a larger hat with your hands)
> Here's the way he folds his arms,
>   (fold your arms abruptly)
> And takes a little nap.
>   (close your eyes and snore)

WHAT YOUR TODDLER WILL LEARN:
Language skills

A little ball

◆ Here is a popular poem by an unknown author. Recite the poem and move your arms to illustrate the poem while your toddler copies you.

> A little ball,
>   (clasp your hands together into a ball)
> A bigger ball,
>   (move your hands apart, curving them into a
>   ball shape)
> A great big ball I see.
>   (stretch your arms and hands up into a wide arc)
> Now let's count the balls,
> One,
>   (stretch your hands and arms up into a wide arc)
> Two,
>   (curve your hands into a ball shape)
> Three.
>   (clasp your hands together)

WHAT YOUR TODDLER WILL LEARN:

Language skills

Art and Singing Games

I see something

◆ Collect a ball and a toy car, both of the same colour.

◆ Sing to the tune of "Frère Jacques".

> *I see something, I see something*
> *Used to play, used to play.*
> *It is very round,*
> *You can roll it over,*
> *What is it? What is it?*
>
> *I see something, I see something;*
> *It can go, it can go.*
> *It is (green) and shiny,*
> *And the horn goes "beep beep".*
> *What is it? What is it?*

◆ Urge your child to answer your question, "What is it?" by pointing out or picking up the object about which you've been singing.

◆ This is a wonderful game for nonverbal children because all they have to do is point to an object.

◆ Adapt this song by making up lyrics to fit other things in your baby's environment.

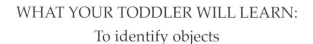

WHAT YOUR TODDLER WILL LEARN:
To identify objects

The singing ball

◆ Hold a beach ball in your hand. It should be small enough for your toddler to hold easily because he will want to try this game on his own.

◆ Bounce the ball once, saying, "Bounce."

◆ Keep bouncing the ball while you say:

> *Bounce, bounce,*
> *One, two.*
> *Bounce, bounce,*
> *Three, four.*
> *Bounce, bounce,*
> *Bounce, bounce,*
> *One, two, three, four.*

◆ Make up a sing-song melody to the words. Repeat the song and see whether your child can sing with you.

◆ Give the ball to your child and let him try the game.

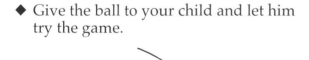

WHAT YOUR TODDLER WILL LEARN:
Counting

Scribbling game

◆ Giving your toddler plenty of crayons, markers, pencils and chalk will encourage him to scribble. Scribbling develops hand–eye coordination, which is important in a young child's development.

◆ Supervised scribbling can be great fun for you and your child.

◆ Sit at a table with your toddler. Spread drawing paper on the table. Show him how to place the crayon on the paper and move his hand back and forth.

◆ Praise the lines and squiggles that he makes. Tell him how pretty the picture is, noting a specific feature, for example, "I really like the round red lines in your picture."

◆ With a crayon, draw an interesting shape and say, "I made a picture. Can you make a picture?"

◆ Games like these are very fulfilling to toddlers and develop their self-esteem.

WHAT YOUR TODDLER WILL LEARN:
Hand–eye coordination

Where is it?

◆ Play this game in one room at a time.

◆ Walk around the room with your toddler, naming objects. Speak in short, clear sentences: "This is a chair; this is a piano; this is the door."

◆ Then ask your toddler, "Where is the chair?"

◆ Continue asking about each object that you named.

WHAT YOUR TODDLER WILL LEARN:
Observation skills

Cha, cha, cha

◆ Place marbles or other objects that make interesting sounds inside a metal tin.

◆ Tape the lid securely, making sure there are no sharp edges.

◆ Give the tin to your toddler and encourage him to shake it while you both sing.

◆ Sing a familiar tune like "Old MacDonald had a farm".

◆ Next, in a sing-song voice, sing the words, "One, two, cha, cha, cha."

◆ Show your child how to shake the tin on "cha, cha, cha".

◆ Repeat several times. Soon your toddler will understand to shake the tin on "cha, cha, cha".

WHAT YOUR TODDLER WILL LEARN:
Rhythm

Head and shoulders

◆ Recite this poem with your child, first touching the part of the body named on yourself, then on your toddler:

> *Head and shoulders, knees and toes,*
> *Knees and toes.*
> *Head and shoulders, knees and toes,*
> *Knees and toes.*
> *Eyes and ears and mouth and nose.*
> *Head and shoulders, knees and toes,*
> *Knees and toes.*

◆ After you have played this game a while, see whether she can touch the parts of her body as you recite.

◆ Another variation is to give her a doll to see whether she can identify those parts of the doll's body.

◆ Sing to the tune of "There's a tavern in the town".

WHAT YOUR TODDLER WILL LEARN:
Body awareness

Boat rowing

◆ Sit on the floor facing your toddler.

◆ Spread her knees slightly apart and place your legs over hers. Grasp her hands and begin to pull back and forth. Lean forward until her back touches the floor, then bring her back up.

◆ Sing while you play this game.

> *Row, row, row your boat,*
> *Gently down the stream.*
> *Merrily, merrily, merrily, merrily,*
> *Life is but a dream.*

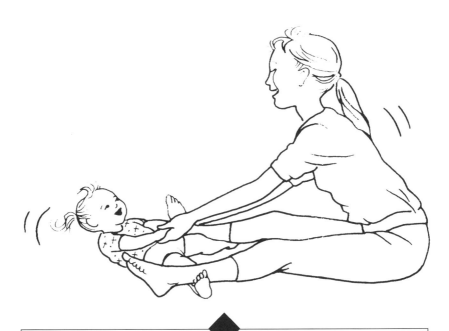

WHAT YOUR TODDLER WILL LEARN:

Coordination

Jingle bell songs

◆ Bells are a wonderful accompaniment to songs. A music or school supply or crafts shop will have a variety of bells.

◆ The song "Jingle bells" is very popular. Your toddler can shake the bells as you sing.

◆ Another nice song for bells is the nursery rhyme "Hey, diddle, diddle". Shake the bells at the beginning of each line.

> *Hey, diddle, diddle,*
> *The cat and the fiddle,*
> *The cow jumped over the moon.*
> *The little dog laughed*
> *To see such sport,*
> *And the dish ran away with the spoon.*

◆ Experiment with fast and slow shaking.

WHAT YOUR TODDLER WILL LEARN:
Rhythm

The shape game

◆ You will need a large sheet of drawing paper and a crayon.

◆ Sit with your child at a table or on the floor.

◆ Draw a circle on the paper with the crayon. Then put the crayon in the child's hand and guide her hand in making a circle. Say to her, "What a pretty picture."

◆ Guide your toddler's hand to draw a different shape. Again say, "What a pretty picture."

◆ Experiment with zigzag lines, free movement, etc.

◆ Toddlers love this game and, interestingly enough, want to take turns. Your child will probably give the crayon to you and say, "You do it."

◆ Each time that you play, it's a good idea to use a crayon of a different colour so she begins to identify colours.

◆ Use the "fat" crayons that are easier for little hands to hold.

WHAT YOUR TODDLER WILL LEARN:
Creativity

This old man

◆ This is a wonderful spoon-banging song. When you sing, "This old man came rolling home," roll your toddler's fists one over the other.

> *This old man, he played one,*
> *He played nick-nack on my thumb.*
> *With a nick-nack, paddy-whack,*
> *Give a dog a bone,*
> *This old man came rolling home.*

◆ Sing all ten verses, making these substitutions in the first and second lines:

> *Two—on my shoe*
> *Three—on my knee*
> *Four—on my door*
> *Five—on a hive*
> *Six—on some sticks*
> *Seven—all the way to Heaven*
> *Eight—on my gate*
> *Nine—on my spine*
> *Ten—once again*

WHAT YOUR TODDLER WILL LEARN:
Counting

If you're happy

◆ The song "If you're happy and you know it" is wonderful for teaching parts of the body to toddlers.

> *If you're happy and you know it, clap your hands.*
> *If you're happy and you know it, clap your hands.*
> *If you're happy and you know it,*
> *Then your smile will surely show it.*
> *If you're happy and you know it, clap your hands.*

◆ For other verses, snap your fingers, wave your hands, tap your feet, shake your foot, wiggle your ears, touch your nose—and anything else that you choose.

◆ Try singing this song to accompany motor activities:

> *If you're happy and you know it, jump up and down.*
> *If you're happy and you know it, turn around.*
> *If you're happy and you know it, bend your knees.*

◆ Use this song to express feelings:

> *If you're sad and you know it, cry like me.*
> *If you're happy and you know it, laugh out loud.*

WHAT YOUR TODDLER WILL LEARN:

Body awareness

The two feet game

◆ Hold your toddler's hand while you recite and act out this rhyme:

> *I can walk with two feet, two feet, two feet.*
> *I can walk with two feet, all day long.*

◆ Try other ways of moving your feet:

> *I can jump with two feet...*
> *I can hop with two feet...*
> *I can run with two feet...*
> *I can march with two feet...*
> *I can slide with two feet...*
> *I can skip with two feet...*

◆ Move other parts of the body:

> *I can blink with two eyes...*
> *I can shake with one head...*
> *I can wiggle ten fingers...*

WHAT YOUR TODDLER WILL LEARN:
Coordination

Down by the station

◆ Sing "Down by the station" with your toddler. Place your hands on his waist and pretend the two of you are a choo-choo train.

> *Down by the station,*
> *Early in the morning,*
> *See the little puffer bellies*
> *All in a row.*
> *See the station master*
> *Turn the little handle,*
> *Chug chug, toot toot,*
> *Off we go.*

◆ Sing the song three times, faster each time. Then sing twice more, slower each time. The last time, change the final two lines to "Chug chug, toot toot, home they go."

WHAT YOUR TODDLER WILL LEARN:
Listening skills

Art outdoors

◆ Take a baking pan filled with sand or salt outside.

◆ Encourage your toddler to draw in the pan with his fingers. When he tires of his drawings, shake the pan to erase them.

◆ Bring an easel, paint, paper and brushes outdoors. Suggest your child experiment with painting on the easel. When his painting is finished, hang it up to dry.

◆ Fill a plastic tray with whipped topping and let your toddler fingerpaint with it. He may lick his fingers as a final treat.

WHAT YOUR TODDLER WILL LEARN:
Imaginative play

Instrument fun

◆ Make two paper bag shakers, one for your child and one for yourself. Decorate the paper bags with magic marker and fill them with a little rice or a few dried beans.

◆ Tie the bags securely and give them to your child.

◆ Show her how to shake the bags to music.

◆ Sing favourite songs while you shake the bags.

◆ Play music of varying tempos and styles, such as marches, waltzes or something with a Spanish flair.

WHAT YOUR TODDLER WILL LEARN:
Rhythm

Ring-a-ring o'roses

◆ This game is a great favourite among toddlers.

> *Ring-a-ring o'roses,*
> *A pocket full of posies;*
> *Atishoo, atishoo,*
> *We all fall down.*
> *BOOM!*

◆ If your child can walk, hold his hands while you walk in a circle, then fall down.

◆ If your child cannot walk, hold him and walk in a circle. Instead of falling down, sit gently down on a chair.

◆ Another version is:

> *Ring-a-ring o'roses,*
> *A pocket full of posies;*
> *Atishoo, atishoo,*
> *All jump up.*
> *HEY!*

"BOOM!" and "HEY!" are favourite parts of this game.

WHAT YOUR TODDLER WILL LEARN:
Bonding

The shadow game

◆ Go for a walk outside on a sunny day to look for shadows.

◆ Look at your own shadow. Move your arms, jump up and down, jump on your toddler's shadow. Talk about how the shadow got there.

◆ Sing to the tune of "The muffin man" while watching your shadow:

> *Oh, do you see my shadow go,*
> *My shadow go, my shadow go?*
> *Oh, do you see my shadow go?*
> *It goes along with me.*
>
> *Oh, do you see my shadow bend,*
> *My shadow bend, my shadow bend?*
> *Oh, do you see my shadow bend?*
> *It bends along with me.*

◆ Sing two more verses using these lines:

> *Oh, do you see my shadow jump.*
> *Oh, do you see my shadow run.*

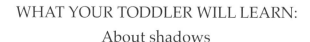

WHAT YOUR TODDLER WILL LEARN:

About shadows

Paint with your feet

◆ Spread a large sheet of paper outside.

◆ Set big sponges in a large, shallow tray next to the paper. Pour tempera paint on to the sponges.

◆ Use your feet as paintbrushes. Hold your child's hand and show her how to dip one foot into the paint. Walk across the paper, holding your toddler's hand in case it's a little slippery.

◆ Try this with several different colours of paint, or put paint on a ball and roll it across the paper, or make hand prints.

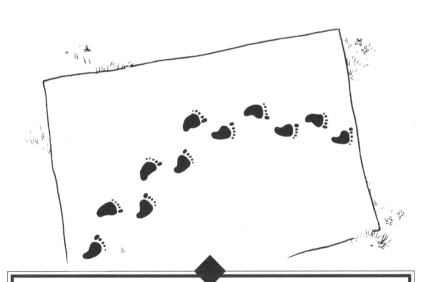

WHAT YOUR TODDLER WILL LEARN:
Coordination

The post is here

◆ Your toddler will enjoy investigating the post, tearing it, looking at pictures and examining different shapes and sizes.

◆ Before you throw away that junk mail, why not use it to develop your toddler's language skills and coordination?

◆ Opening envelopes is great fun for toddlers. If he is unable to, open the envelopes yourself and let him take the post out.

◆ The envelopes are full of treasures: beautiful pictures, many textures of paper, different shapes and sizes. All of these are stimulating discoveries for your child.

◆ Pretend to be the postman and say to your child, "The post is here, and I have some letters for you. Let's see who they are from."

◆ Pretend to read the letters from Grandma, Uncle Harry and other family members that your child will recognize.

WHAT YOUR TODDLER WILL LEARN:
Language skills

Puppet songs

◆ Collect several tongue depressors. Put a sticker on the end of each one. Help your toddler do this.

◆ If you have animal stickers, sing "Old MacDonald had a farm" and pretend the sticker puppets are singing.

◆ Let your toddler dance the puppets around as you sing to the tune of "Frère Jacques".

> *Where's the puppet, where's the puppet?*
> *Here I am, here I am.*
> *I can go up high,*
> *I can go down low,*
> *Fly away, fly away.*

◆ Begin and end the poem holding the puppets behind your back. On the second line, bring out the puppets, then raise them high, then lower them.

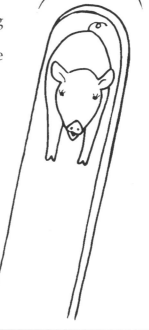

WHAT YOUR TODDLER WILL LEARN:
Play skills

Collage

◆ Gather together lots of odds and ends—paper, junk mail, greeting cards, string, wool, wrapping paper, beans, etc.

◆ Lay a large sheet of heavy paper or cardboard on the table.

◆ Using a glue stick, dab glue on one thing at a time and give them to your child to place on the paper.

◆ Let her select the things she wants you to glue.

◆ Your child can dab on the glue herself as long as she is closely supervised.

◆ Hang the finished collage in a prominent place for everyone to admire.

WHAT YOUR TODDLER WILL LEARN:
Creativity

Working with playdough

◆ Here are some activities for you and your toddler to try with playdough:

- Help your child make balls and snakes.
- Talk about the colours of the playdough. Mix the colours together.
- Form shapes with playdough like circles, triangles and squares.
- Make letters.
- Press or roll the playdough with a rolling pin. Make patterns on the flattened surface with blocks, toys, a comb or stones.
- Cut the playdough with biscuit cutters.

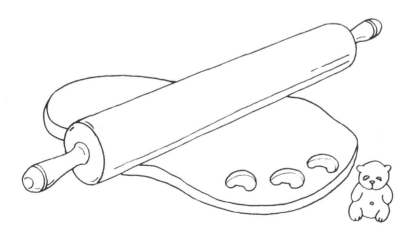

WHAT YOUR TODDLER WILL LEARN:
Creativity

Pumpkin printing

◆ Cut shapes from the rind of a pumpkin: squares, triangles, rectangles, circles and irregular shapes.

◆ Dip the shapes into tempera paint and print designs on large sheets of paper. As you print, name the shape for your toddler.

◆ Give your child a shape. Name the shape, then let her print all over the paper.

◆ Continue printing with the regular shapes. When you use an irregular shape, make up a name for it.

◆ Many fruits and vegetables—carrots, apple slices and potatoes—can be substituted for pumpkin.

◆ Sponges also work well. Cut them into interesting shapes before printing with them.

WHAT YOUR TODDLER WILL LEARN:
Creativity

Silly singing

◆ A favourite children's song is "Yankee Doodle".

◆ Put your child on your lap facing you. Bounce her up and down as you sing.

> *Yankee Doodle went to town,*
> *A riding on a pony,*
> *Stuck a feather in his cap*
> *And called it macaroni.*

◆ Ask your child, "Where's the macaroni?" Touch her head and say, "Here it is!"

◆ Sing the song again, but instead of saying "macaroni", name another kind of food, such as sausages, that your toddler likes.

WHAT YOUR TODDLER WILL LEARN:
Language skills

The sticker game

◆ Toddlers love stickers! Make a special card to send to a friend, to grandparents or to each other.

◆ Select stickers that have the same shape. Geometric shapes are particularly nice because they help the child identify squares, circles, etc.

◆ Print something simple on an A4 sheet of paper, for example, "Dear Grandpa, I love you."

◆ Tell your child what the words say, then let her decorate the paper with stickers. You may have to show her how.

◆ Once you are finished, post the card to the person to whom it was written.

WHAT YOUR TODDLER WILL LEARN:
Socialization skills

Find the other one

◆ Play a matching game with pairs of things: shoes, mittens, coloured napkins, towels, flannels, etc.

◆ Mix up a few pairs and help your child find the ones that match.

◆ Sing to the tune of "Frère Jacques":

> *I have a mitten, I have a mitten.*
> *It is red, it is red.*
> *Help me find the other one.*
> *Help me find the other one.*
> *Here it is, here it is.*
>
> *I have a shoe, I have a shoe.*
> *It is brown, it is brown.*
> *Help me find the other one.*
> *Help me find the other one.*
> *Here it is, here it is.*
>
> *I have a napkin, I have a napkin.*
> *It is yellow, it is yellow.*
> *Help me find the other one.*
> *Help me find the other one.*
> *Here it is, here it is.*

◆ Sing the song about each item that you match.

WHAT YOUR TODDLER WILL LEARN:
Matching skills

Instruments make music

◆ Creating simple rhythm instruments will thrill your toddler and make singing more fun.

◆ Drums can be made from a round box. Cover the open end with adhesive-backed plastic. Put a rubber band over the plastic around the rim to be sure that it is secure. The smaller the box, the higher pitched the sound; the larger the box, the lower the sound.

◆ Make shakers by putting stones, beads or buttons inside film canisters. Securely fasten the lids.

◆ Play your instruments while you sing a favourite song.

WHAT YOUR TODDLER WILL LEARN:
Rhythm

Where is Thumbkin?

◆ Sing this popular fingerplay to the tune of "Frère Jacques":

> *Where is Thumbkin, where is Thumbkin?*
> *(hide your hands behind your back)*
> *Here I am, here I am.*
> *(show your hands with thumbs up)*
> *How are you today, sir?*
> *(shake one hand)*
> *Very well, I thank you.*
> *(shake the other hand)*
> *Run away, run away.*
> *(put your hands behind your back)*

◆ Sing five more verses, substituting for Thumbkin your index, middle, ring and little finger, and finally, your entire hand:

> *Where is Pointer?*
> *Where is Middle Finger?*
> *Where is Ring Finger?*
> *Where is Little Finger?*
> *Where's the whole family?*

WHAT YOUR TODDLER WILL LEARN:
Coordination

Wiggling toes

◆ Take off your shoes and your toddler's.

◆ Show your child how to wiggle his toes.

◆ Sing to the tune of "The bear went over the mountain".

> *Oh, my toes are starting to wiggle,*
> *My toes are starting to wiggle,*
> *My toes are starting to wiggle,*
> *Wiggling all day long.*

◆ Continue singing about your legs, hips, shoulders, elbows, hands, head and anything else you wish to include. This is a great way to teach parts of the body.

WHAT YOUR TODDLER WILL LEARN:

Body awareness

Car Games

Do you see?

◆ While riding in the car, point out things to your child.

◆ Encourage him to look out the window and observe.

◆ Sing to the tune of "The muffin man" to direct his attention:

> *Oh, do you see a pretty car,*
> *A pretty car, a pretty car?*
> *Oh, do you see a pretty car,*
> *Can you tell me yes?*
>
> *Oh, yes, I see a pretty car,*
> *A pretty car, a pretty car.*
> *Oh, yes, I see a pretty car,*
> *Yes, yes, yes.*

◆ As you point to a car, say, "There it is."

◆ Sing about other things that you see through the window.

WHAT YOUR TODDLER WILL LEARN:
Observation skills

Who is riding?

◆ Sing to the tune of "London Bridge is falling down":

> *Who is riding in the car,*
> *In the car, in the car?*
> *Who is riding in the car?*
> *It is Mummy.*

◆ Repeat the song, naming other family members like Daddy, Grandma, Aunt Mary, etc. Talk about the places you go in the car, like the supermarket, the park, etc.

◆ On the last line, sing about a place:

> *Daddy's riding in the car,*
> *In the car, in the car.*
> *Daddy's riding in the car,*
> *To the park.*

WHAT YOUR TODDLER WILL LEARN:
Language skills

A driving we will go

◆ Sing to the tune of "A-hunting we will go":

> *Oh, a driving we will go,*
> *A driving we will go,*
> *A driving we will go, go, go*
> *A driving we will go.*

◆ After singing, ask, "Who can we drive in the car to see?" Whatever the child responds, make up a story to go with it: "We will drive to Grandma's house and play in the garden," or, "We will drive to the market to buy some food."

◆ Depending on your child's age, expand the story using familiar experiences.

◆ Try extending the story by asking your child questions: "When we finish playing at Grandma's, where shall we go?"

◆ Give your child ideas: "Shall we go into the house and give Grandma a hug?"

◆ Another way to adapt this song is to turn it into a motor activity. Instead of driving, run, hop, jump, etc. Not in the car of course!

WHAT YOUR TODDLER WILL LEARN:
Imaginative play

Travelling music

◆ Music is fun while riding in the car. Sing favourite songs or listen to your toddler's most loved tapes.

◆ If your child knows a nursery rhyme or song well, sing it leaving out a word. For example, "Baa, baa, black sheep, have you any _____? Yes, sir, yes, sir, three bags _____."

◆ Once your toddler can fill in the missing word, show him how to change its sound by singing loudly or softly.

◆ Try singing a familiar song with a word left out of the middle of a sentence instead of the end.

WHAT YOUR TODDLER WILL LEARN:
Language skills

Looking out of the window

◆ This game helps toddlers look for specific things while riding in a car. Recite this rhyme:

> *I'm looking out the window,*
> *I'm looking out the window,*
> *I'm looking out the window,*
> *And this is what I see.*

◆ After you say, "And this is what I see," call out in a big voice, "I see a car." Then ask your toddler, "Do you see the car?"

◆ The basic purpose of this game is to direct your toddler's attention. Repeat the rhyme and direct your toddler's attention to other objects like the street, people, animals, colours, etc.

WHAT YOUR TODDLER WILL LEARN:

Language skills

Car puppets

◆ This game keeps your child occupied in the car while it develops his language.

◆ Draw a face on each of your child's thumbs with a felt-tipped pen.

◆ Name the thumb puppets so that you can talk to them: "Hello, funny face," or, "How are you, Billy?"

◆ As you drive, talk to the thumb puppets. Your toddler can talk back or just move his thumbs up and down in reply.

◆ Here are a few things to say to the puppets.

> *Do you see that red car?*
> *Look at the beautiful trees.*
> *Red light stop; green light go.*

◆ Ask the puppets to join you in singing familiar songs.

WHAT YOUR TODDLER WILL LEARN:
Language skills

This is the way

◆ Driving in the car can be wonderfully educational for your toddler. He can learn about parts of the car and what they do.

◆ Sing to the tune of "Here we go 'round the mulberry bush":

> *This is the way we drive the car,*
> *Drive the car, drive the car.*
> *This is the way we drive the car,*
> *Every single day.*
>
> *This is the way we honk the horn,*
> *Honk the horn, honk the horn.*
> *This is the way we honk the horn,*
> *Every single day.*

◆ On the first line, pretend to turn the steering wheel, and in the second verse, pretend to honk the horn.

◆ Sing more verses about the car.

> *This is the way we open the door…*
> *This is the way the wipers go…*
> *This is the way we turn the key…*
> *This is the way we lock the doors…*
> *This is the way the seat belt goes…*
> *This is the way we stop the car…*

WHAT YOUR TODDLER WILL LEARN:
Language skills

Peek-a-boo car

◆ Peek-a-boo is a great game that children seem to enjoy until about age three.

◆ This version is ideal for the car and will keep your toddler occupied as well as sharpen his visual skills.

◆ Play peek-a-boo with parts of the car. Tell your toddler to cover his eyes and play peek-a-boo with the steering wheel.

◆ Keep suggesting different parts of the car: the wipers, the radio, the window, etc. Then explore what you see out of the window: "Play peek-a-boo with that lady," or, "Play peek-a-boo with the bridge."

◆ Ask your toddler, "Where is the sun? Can you play peek-a-boo with the sun?"

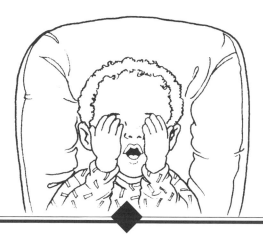

WHAT YOUR TODDLER WILL LEARN:
Fun

Car pockets

◆ Sew several pockets on a pillowcase using scraps of material or felt.

◆ From additional felt, cut shapes and figures of animals and people small enough to fit into the pockets. Decorate the cutouts.

◆ Give your toddler the pillowcase while riding in the car. He will enjoy playing with the animals and people.

◆ Before you start driving, show your child how to hide the felt pieces in the pockets, and how to peek their heads out.

◆ If you reserve this game only for the car, your toddler will become very excited whenever he sees it.

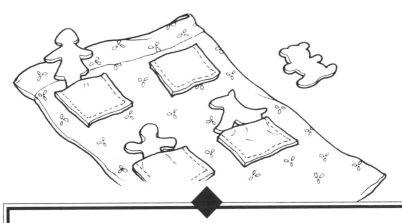

WHAT YOUR TODDLER WILL LEARN:
Play skills

Red and green

◆ Driving in the car with your toddler is a perfect time to teach about red and green lights.

◆ Sing to the tune of "The farmer's in his den":

> *I'm driving in the car.*
> *I'm driving in the car.*
> *Beep, beep, beep, beep,*
> *I'm driving in the car.*
>
> *The light is turning red.*
> *The light is turning red.*
> *Stop, stop, stop, stop,*
> *The light is turning red.*
>
> *The light is turning green.*
> *The light is turning green.*
> *Go, go, go, go,*
> *The light is turning green.*

◆ Since your toddler is just learning to recognize colours, this game is even more fun for him.

WHAT YOUR TODDLER WILL LEARN:
About colours

Old MacDonald had a car

◆ Riding in the car is a wonderful time to share music and fun.

◆ Here is a new version of a familiar song:

> *Old MacDonald had a car,*
> *E I E I O.*
> *And on his car he had a horn,*
> *E I E I O.*
> *With a beep, beep here, and a beep, beep there.*
> *Here a beep, there a beep,*
> *Everywhere a beep, beep.*
> *Old MacDonald had a car,*
> *E I E I O.*

◆ As you sing, your toddler can pretend to honk the horn.

◆ Sing about other parts of the car:

> *Wipers—Swish, swish here, swish, swish there.*
> *Motor—Hrum, hrum here, hrum, hrum there.*
> *Radio—La, la here, la, la there.*

WHAT YOUR TODDLER WILL LEARN:
Fun

Toot the horn

◆ Talk about the equipment in the car and what each thing does:

> *Horn honks.*
> > *(pretend to honk the horn)*
> *Wheel turns.*
> > *(pretend to turn the wheel)*
> *Wipers swish.*
> > *(move your hands like the wipers)*
> *Windows go up and down.*
> > *(move your hands up and down)*

◆ Sing to the tune of "Here we go 'round the mulberry bush" and pretend to honk the horn:

> *This is the way we honk the horn,*
> *Honk the horn, honk the horn.*
> *This is the way we honk the horn,*
> *While riding in the car.*

◆ Continue singing additional verses:

> *This is the way we turn the wheel...*
> *This is the way we open the door...*
> *This is the way we step on the brake...*

WHAT YOUR TODDLER WILL LEARN:
Language skills

Car talk

◆ Riding in the car with your child is a perfect time for a special game together.

◆ As you drive, describe to your toddler the things that you do. For example, "Now I'm putting my foot on the brake, and the car stops."

◆ The next time you stop, repeat the same explanation and encourage your toddler to say, "Stop."

◆ Toddlers love to watch the windscreen wipers. Say to your child, "Now I'm going to turn on the wipers."

◆ This kind of conversation will also develop thinking and language skills.

WHAT YOUR TODDLER WILL LEARN:
Thinking skills

Telephone time

◆ Car phones are so popular these days, that a toy phone in the car seems natural.

◆ While your toddler sits in his car seat, suggest he call someone.

◆ Tell him where you are going and ask him to call ahead: "Call Grandma and tell her that we will be there soon." Give him an idea of what to say: "Hello, Grandma, we'll be there in five minutes."

◆ Whether you are going to the supermarket, to the park or to pick up someone from school, pretend to call them from the car.

◆ After a few times, your child will have his own ideas of what to say.

WHAT YOUR TODDLER WILL LEARN:
Language skills

Mary had a little car

◆ Sing to the tune of "Mary had a little lamb":

> *[Child's name] had a little car, little car, little car.*
> *[Child's name] had a little car,*
> *And the horn went beep, beep, beep.*

◆ Sing the song using your toddler's name. Pretend to honk a horn when you sing "beep, beep, beep".

◆ Toddlers love repetition and enjoy singing this song over and over. Try changing the first word: "Daddy had a little car," or, "Grandma had a little car."

◆ Sing about a favourite stuffed animal, a pet or a friend.

◆ Try changing the sound of the horn. Sing "honk" or "waa" instead of "beep", or make up your own noise.

WHAT YOUR TODDLER WILL LEARN:
Language skills

Fun talk

◆ Riding in the car is a perfect time for wonderful conversations with your toddler to develop her language.

◆ Point out familiar things to her. When she repeats one word, repeat her word in a complete sentence. If she says, "Dog," reply, "That's a brown dog," or, "Yes, that's a big dog."

◆ Name items in the car: door, wheel, wipers, etc. Each time she repeats a word, expand that word into a sentence.

◆ Your toddler is soaking up this information which will later help her construct her own sentences.

WHAT YOUR TODDLER WILL LEARN:
Language skills

21-24

Lookie, lookie

◆ Make a toy for the car from the cardboard tube of a paper towel roll.

◆ Show your toddler how to look through the tube.

◆ Ask the child to find a certain object. When he finds it, ask him to say, "Lookie, lookie, I see a _____." For example:

Adult: "Can you find something red?"
Child: "Lookie, lookie, I see a red _____."
Adult: "Can you find something tall?"
Child: "Lookie, lookie, I see a tall_____."

◆ Toddlers love to say, "Lookie, lookie." (I think it's because it sounds like "cookie".)

◆ Play this game to teach him about the car: "Can you find the wipers?" or, "Can you find the wheel?"

WHAT YOUR TODDLER WILL LEARN:
Observation skills

Games to Play with Toddlers

Special Bonding Games

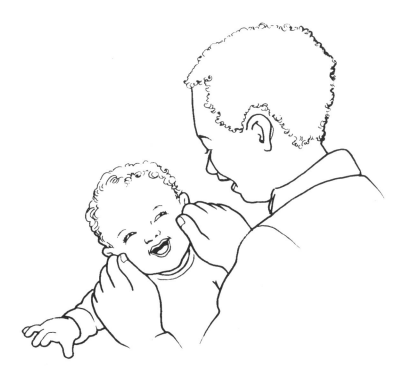

Colour walk

◆ Take a colour walk with your toddler. Select a toy of a certain colour to bring with you.

◆ Find one or two objects in each room of the same colour as the toy.

◆ Talk about what you've found. For example, "Daddy's yellow tie is the same colour as your yellow ball," or, "Mummy's blue blouse is the same colour as your blue block."

◆ A variation of this game is to carry a laundry basket around, collecting toys and other objects of the same colour.

WHAT YOUR TODDLER WILL LEARN:
About colours

Baby bunny

◆ Recite the poem and act out the bunny with your hands and fingers.

◆ Hold up your index and middle finger for the bunny ears. Bend your thumb, ring finger and little finger into your palm. (You are making a V with your hand.)

Here are the baby bunny ears.
    (hold up the bunny ears)
And here is his little pink nose.
    (touch your thumb)
This is the way he hippity hops,
    (hop the bunny)
Everywhere he goes.

This is the way the baby bunny crawls,
    (crawl bunny up to your chin)
Shuts his eyes and goes to sleep,
    (close your eyes)
With his little feet tucked in.
    (pat the bunny)

WHAT YOUR TODDLER WILL LEARN:
Fun

Book sounds

◆ Play with your toddler's animal toys to help him learn new sounds.

◆ Show him an animal toy, name it and make its sound.

◆ Show a picture of the same animal, name it and make its sound.

◆ Point to the toy and ask, "What does the doggie say?"etc. (It is better to ask, "What does the animal say?" than "How does the animal go?")

◆ Look through magazines with your child to find pictures of familiar animals. Cut them out and put them on cardboard to make your own animal book.

WHAT YOUR TODDLER WILL LEARN:
About animals

Animal sounds

◆ Toddlers really enjoy making animal sounds.

◆ Gather together a group of plastic toy animals. Show your toddler an animal and tell her the sound that it makes.

◆ Ask her to copy you and make the animal sound, too.

◆ After you have looked at three or four animals and made their sounds, match the toy to a picture of the same animal.

◆ Show your child a picture and ask her to find the matching toy and make its sound.

WHAT YOUR TODDLER WILL LEARN:
About animals

I have

◆ The more your toddler learns about his body, the more he will understand what it can do.

◆ Recite this poem with your toddler, acting out the lines:

I have two eyes to see with,
    (touch your eyes with your hands)
I have two feet to run,
    (run in place)
I have two hands to wave with,
    (wave both hands)
 But a nose, I have but one.
    (touch your nose)
I have two ears to hear with,
    (touch your ears)
And a tongue to say "hello",
    (point to your tongue)
And two red cheeks for you to pinch,
    (gently pinch your
    toddler's cheeks)
And now it's time to go.
    (run around the
    room)

WHAT YOUR TODDLER WILL LEARN:
Body awareness

Baby-o

◆ Bounce your toddler up and down on your lap as you recite this poem:

> *What will we do with the baby-o?*
> *What will we do with the baby-o?*
> *What will we do with the baby-o?*
> *Send him to his Daddy-o.*
> > *(holding the baby firmly, let him bounce down between your knees)*
>
> *What will we do with the baby-o?*
> *What will we do with the baby-o?*
> *What will we do with the baby-o?*
> *Send him to his Mummy-o.*
> > *(lift him up for a big hug)*

◆ The third time, instead of saying "baby-o", substitute your child's name with an "o" added on the end. On the last line say, "Tickle his little tummy-o."

WHAT YOUR TODDLER WILL LEARN:
Trust

Sharing game

◆ Sit on the floor opposite your baby.

◆ Give the baby an object like a favourite toy and say, "This is for you."

◆ After your baby has had a chance to touch, look and explore it, say, "Will you give it back to me, please?"

◆ The baby will give you the toy.

◆ Repeat the game.

WHAT YOUR TODDLER WILL LEARN:
To share

Two little dickey birds

◆ Recite this poem, carrying out the actions with your thumb and encouraging your toddler to follow your actions:

> *Two little dickey birds, sitting on a hill,*
>   *(close your hands and stick up your thumbs)*
> *One named Jack,*
>   *(bring your right thumb forward)*
> *And one named Jill.*
>   *(bring your left thumb forward)*
> *Fly away, Jack.*
>   *(wave your right thumb like a flying bird and hide it behind your back)*
> *Fly away, Jill.*
>   *(wave your left thumb and hide it behind your back)*
> *Come back, Jack.*
>   *(bring your right thumb back into view)*
> *Come back, Jill.*
>   *(bring your left thumb back)*

◆ Try wetting your thumbs and sticking small pieces of tissue paper to them, to make them look like birds.

◆ Finger puppets are also nice for acting out this rhyme.

WHAT YOUR TODDLER WILL LEARN:
Imitation

Wiggle worm

◆ Sit on the floor with your baby facing you. Recite this poem, wiggling your toes, then stopping on the last line:

> *Wiggle your toes, one, two, three.*
> *Wiggle your toes just like me.*
> *Now tell the wiggles to go away,*
> *And sit very still for the rest of the day.*

◆ When you say "go away", shake your index finger.

◆ Repeat the poem substituting different parts of the body: fingers, elbows, nose, ears and tongue.

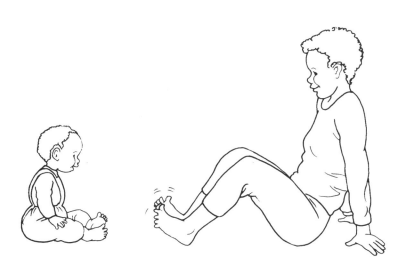

WHAT YOUR TODDLER WILL LEARN:

Body awareness

Somersaults

◆ You will need a soft yet firm surface for these first somersaults. Be sure it is safe enough should your toddler try it when you are not in the room.

◆ Ask your child to look at her tummy or belly button. She will tuck her head down to do so. Very gently push her head down towards her chest.

◆ Hold and lift her hips slightly as you guide her into a forwardr oll.

◆ Be certain her back is rounded and her chin very close to her chest.

◆ Continue doing somersaults. Each time, as you prepare to roll her forwards, say, "On your marks, get set, GO!"

WHAT YOUR TODDLER WILL LEARN:
Coordination

Look closely

◆ Sit at a table with your toddler and tell him that you want to do something special.

◆ Holding an orange in your hand, talk about its name and colour.

◆ Give the orange to your child. Ask him to smell the orange and feel it with his hand. Talk about the smell and feel.

◆ Peel and open the orange. Show the sections to your child. Give him a section and show him its membrane and seeds.

◆ Eat a section and ask your child if he would like a taste, too.

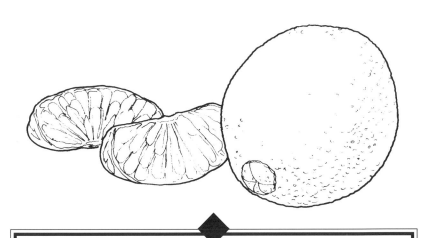

WHAT YOUR TODDLER WILL LEARN:
Observation skills

Torchlight fun

◆ Shine a torch on different parts of the room: the wall, door, floor, under the covers, etc.

◆ Each time you shine the light on an object, name it: "This is the wall," or, "This is the doorknob."

◆ Show your child how to turn the torch on and off.

◆ Let your toddler shine the torch on an object and tell you its name.

◆ Give your child directions: "Shine the light on the ceiling," or, "Shine the light on the window." He will understand what you are saying, even though he might not be able to say the words himself.

◆ To create a bird shadow on the wall, cross your wrists with your palms facing you. Extend your fingers to make wings and touch the balls of your thumbs together to form the bird's head.

◆ Move your hands to make the bird "fly".

◆ Look at pictures in a book or a magazine with the torch.

WHAT YOUR TODDLER WILL LEARN:
Thinking skills

Foot fun

◆ Play this game outside on a nice day.

◆ Fill a small plastic tub with water and add a very small amount of liquid soap.

◆ Ask your toddler to take off her shoes and socks all by herself. Tell her that you are going to play a special game with her feet.

◆ Dip your hand into the soapy water and massage some on to one of her feet.

◆ As you massage, touch and talk about different parts of the foot: toes, ankle, heel, arch, sole and skin.

◆ Dry her foot thoroughly. Repeat the same thing with the other foot.

WHAT YOUR TODDLER WILL LEARN:

Body awareness

Margery Daw

◆ Sit on the floor with your toddler facing you. Place your legs over his knees.

◆ Hold your child's hands and seesaw back and forth, reciting this rhyme:

> *Seesaw, Margery Daw,*
> *Jackie shall have a new master.*
> *Jackie shall earn but a penny a day,*
> *Because he can't work any faster.*

◆ The further that you lean in each direction, the better exercise it will be for both of you.

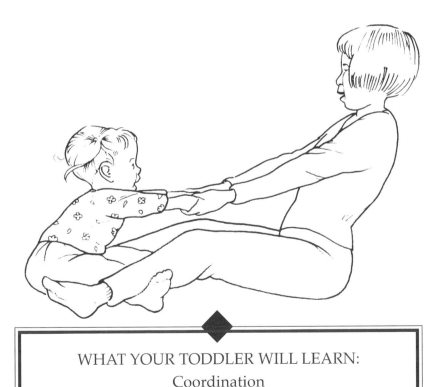

WHAT YOUR TODDLER WILL LEARN:
Coordination

Pony girl

◆ Seat your toddler on your knees facing you.

◆ Hold her hands as you roll your legs side to side and sing:

> *Pony girl,*
> *Won't you be my pony girl?*
> *Hurry up, hop on board.*

◆ Substitute "boy" or your child's name for "girl".

◆ Holding your child's hands securely, bounce your legs up and down and sing:

> *Giddy up, giddy up,*
> *Ride my pony today.*

◆ Repeat twice more. At the end of the third time say, "Whoa," and stop.

WHAT YOUR TODDLER WILL LEARN:

Fun

Incy Wincy Spider

◆ Recite the poem "Incy Wincy Spider" and teach your toddler how to use his hands and arms to act it out.

> *Incy Wincy Spider went up the water spout,*
> *(make your fingers crawl like a spider in the air)*
> *Down came the rain and washed the spider out.*
> *(make your fingers go downwards like rain falling)*
> *Out came the sun and dried up all the rain,*
> *(make a big circle with your arms)*
> *And Incy Wincy Spider went up the spout again.*
> *(crawl your fingers upwards again)*

◆ Demonstrate for your child and he will soon be imitating you.

◆ This popular poem also teaches the concepts of "up" and "down".

WHAT YOUR TODDLER WILL LEARN:
Language skills

Where do you think the baby lives?

◆ Sit your toddler on your lap or on the floor facing you.

◆ Hold his palm upwards as you recite this poem:

> *Where do you think the baby lives?*
> *Where do you think the baby lives?*
> *'Round and 'round,*
> *And 'round and 'round,*
> *And up into his house.*

◆ Circle the child's palm with your index finger. When you reach "up into his house", slowly walk your fingers up his arm and tickle his neck.

◆ Switch roles and let your toddler use his hands to act out the poem.

WHAT YOUR TODDLER WILL LEARN:

Fun

Peek-a-boo book

◆ Get a spiral notebook that opens like a book. An A5 notebook is a good size.

◆ Glue pictures of familiar objects to every other page. If the book were open in front of you, the pictures would be glued to the right-hand page.

◆ Cut the pages without any pictures into several horizontal strips, starting with the left edge of the paper and cutting to the spiral.

◆ This enables your toddler to cover the picture on the right with the strips. Look at the book with your toddler. Turn over one strip at a time, gradually revealing more of the picture. Ask your child to guess what the picture is.

WHAT YOUR TODDLER WILL LEARN:
Thinking skills

Feelings

◆ Find pictures of people expressing feelings of happiness, sadness, laughter, crying, etc. Magazines are a good source.

◆ Paste the pictures on cardboard squares. Punch holes in each square and tie them together with ribbon. You have made a special book to share with your toddler.

◆ Look at the pictures with your child and talk about each one.

◆ If you see laughter, laugh out loud and encourage your child to do the same.

◆ If you see crying, pretend to cry and encourage your toddler to do that, too.

◆ It is important that young children feel free to express their feelings.

◆ Your toddler will soon look at this book by himself.

WHAT YOUR TODDLER WILL LEARN:

Socialization skills

Bath and Dressing Games

Chin chopper

♦ Hold your toddler and talk softly to her. Give her an opportunity to talk back.

♦ Play a face-tapping game. Gently tap her chin and say:

> *This is baby's chin chopper,*
> *Chin chopper, chin chopper,*
> *This is baby's chin chopper,*
> *How are you today?*

♦ Tap her other features, saying in turn, "eye peeper", "nose dropper", "mouth eater" and "brow bender".

♦ Make up words for other parts of the body—"finger toucher", "toe wiggler", etc.

WHAT YOUR TODDLER WILL LEARN:
Language skills

Dressing talk

◆ When children are starting to talk, echo the sounds that they make.

◆ By changing the inflection and intensity of your voice, you stimulate their language development.

◆ While dressing your toddler, talk about what you are doing in simple two- or three-word sentences.

◆ For example, while changing her nappy, say things like, "Change, change, change," or, "Nappy off, nappy on."

◆ Change the rhythm of your words. For example, you can say, "Ma, ma, ma, ma, I love you," rapidly or slowly, or create a rhythm that is syncopated or alternates fast and slow, loud and soft.

◆ By repeating your toddler's language and adding a word or two of your own, you help her develop language skills.

WHAT YOUR TODDLER WILL LEARN:
Language skills

Here comes the rain

◆ While you are bathing your child, recite this poem and act out the lines:

> *Here comes the rain,*
> *Splash, splash, splash.*
>   *(splash the bath water)*
> *Here comes the rain,*
> *Drip, drip, drip.*
>   *(drip little droplets on your toddler)*
> *Here comes the rain,*
> *Pitter, patter,*
>   *(flick your fingers in the water)*
> *Get my sweetie clean all over.*
>   *(wash your toddler with a flannel)*

◆ After a few times, let your child act out the poem.

◆ Once your child can perform the actions, encourage him to say the words: "splash, splash, splash", "drip, drip, drip" and "pitter, patter".

WHAT YOUR TODDLER WILL LEARN:

Language skills

Wake up, toes

◆ Play this game with your toddler in the morning. Grasp her toes and shake them gently as you sing to the tune of "Frère Jacques":

> *Wake up, toesies, wake up, toesies,*
> *I love you, I love you.*
> *Can you say good morning?*
> *Can you say good morning?*
> *I love you, I love you.*

◆ Continue singing the song as you wake up other parts of her body:

> *Wake up, fingers...*
> *Wake up, belly button...*
> *Wake up, shoulders...*
> *Wake up, elbows...*
> *Wake up, nose...*

◆ Soon your toddler will move that part of her body even before you touch it.

WHAT YOUR TODDLER WILL LEARN:
Body awareness

Hickory, dickory, dock

◆ "Hickory, dickory, dock" is a wonderful nursery rhyme for bath time:

> *Hickory, dickory, dock,*
> *The mouse ran up the clock.*
> *The clock struck one,*
> *The mouse ran down,*
> *Hickory, dickory, dock.*

◆ With the soap or flannel, slowly move up the toddlers arm as you sing, "The mouse ran up the clock."

◆ While you sing, "The mouse ran down," slide the soap or flannel quickly down the baby's arm, making a small splash in the water.

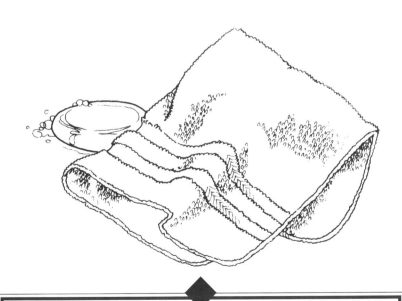

WHAT YOUR TODDLER WILL LEARN:
Bonding

Where's your elbow?

◆ A wonderful time to teach the names of parts of the body is when you are bathing or dressing your toddler.

◆ Touch and name different parts of his body. Ask him to say the name.

◆ Sing to the tune of "Where is Thumbkin?" as you ask for different parts of his body to wash or dress:

> *Where's your elbow, where's your elbow?*
> *Show me now, show me now.*
> *Now I'm going to wash it,*
> *Now I'm going to wash it,*
> *Clean, clean, clean.*
> *Clean, clean, clean.*

◆ If you are singing while dressing your child, change the words to:

> *Now I'm going to dress it,*
> *Now I'm going to dress it,*
> *Dress, dress, dress.*
> *Dress, dress, dress.*

WHAT YOUR TODDLER WILL LEARN:
Body awareness

Body rhyme

◆ Dressing your toddler is a wonderful time to play games that identify and discover what each part of the body can do.

◆ Recite this rhyme while performing the actions:

> *Where are your eyes?*
>   *(touch both eyes with your hands)*
> *Where are your feet?*
>   *(run in place)*
> *Where are your hands?*
>   *(wave your hands in the air)*
> *And your nose so sweet?*
>   *(touch your nose)*
> *Where are your ears?*
>   *(touch both ears with your hands)*
> *Where is your chin?*
>   *(touch your chin)*
> *Where are your cheeks?*
>   *(pinch your toddler's cheeks)*
> *Won't you come in?*
>   *(give your toddler a big hug)*

◆ Repeat the rhyme and encourage your toddler to copy your actions.

WHAT YOUR TODDLER WILL LEARN:
Body awareness

There was a little man

◆ Recite this traditional rhyme with your child while acting out the story:

> *There was a little man who had a little crumb,*
>   *(touch your child's mouth)*
> *And over the mountain he did run.*
>   *(walk your fingers over your toddler's head)*
> *With a belly full of fat,*
>   *(tap his tummy with both hands)*
> *And a big tall hat,*
>   *(raise his hands over his head)*
> *And a pancake stuck to his bum, bum, bum.*
>   *(pat your toddler's bottom)*

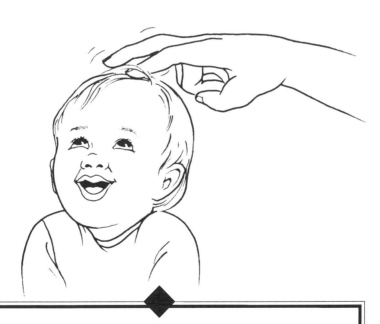

WHAT YOUR TODDLER WILL LEARN:
Fun

Watch the rain

◆ Give a small cup full of water to your toddler while he sits in the bath.

◆ Hold a slotted spoon or colander in front of him, and tell him to pour the water in.

◆ Next let him hold the spoon or colander while you pour the "rain" over it.

◆ Continue playing the game, taking turns pouring the water through the spoon or colander.

◆ As you pour, recite this traditional rhyme:

> *Rain, rain, go away,*
> *Come again another day.*
> *Little _____ [child's name] wants to play.*

WHAT YOUR TODDLER WILL LEARN:
Coordination

Little man in a coal pit

◆ Toddlers often dislike having their shirts pulled over their heads. This rhyme will make it a bit more fun.

◆ First, remove your toddler's arms from the sleeves, then recite the poem, carrying out the actions.

> *Little man in a coal pit,*
> *(hold the shirt up, ready to pull)*
> *Goes knock, knock, knock.*
> *(tap his head gently three times through the shirt)*
> *Up he comes, up he comes*
> *Out at the top.*
> *(pull the shirt off and say, "Hello, little man")*

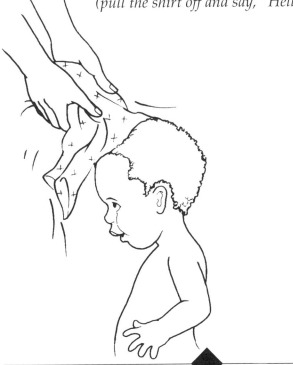

WHAT YOUR TODDLER WILL LEARN:
Dressing skills

Lazy Mary

◆ Sing the song "Lazy Mary, will you get up?":

> *Lazy Mary, will you get up?*
> *Will you get up?*
> *Will you get up?*
> *Lazy Mary, will you get up?*
> *This cold and frosty morning.*

◆ Substitute the name of your toddler for "Mary".

◆ Instead of "lazy", sing words like "pretty", "silly", "funny", "happy", etc.

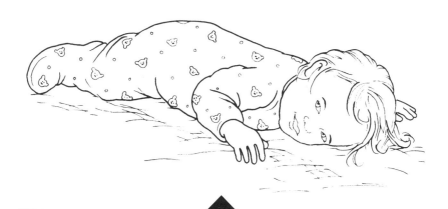

WHAT YOUR TODDLER WILL LEARN:

Language skills

Body stickers

◆ Children at this age enjoy running around nude, particularly after a bath.

◆ This game will help your child become aware of his body.

◆ Get stickers with happy faces or animals that your child recognizes.

◆ Give one to your child and show him how to stick it onto his body.

◆ Tell him to place the sticker on his tummy and push his tummy in and out.

◆ Tell him to place the sticker on his cheek and puff in and out.

◆ Other places to put stickers:

  • Toes—and wiggle them.
  • Elbows—and move them up and down.
  • Palms—and open and close them.

◆

WHAT YOUR TODDLER WILL LEARN:
Body awareness

Bathtime songs

◆ Singing in the bath is great fun for you and your toddler.

◆ Sing the "Hokey cokey" with your child in the bath. This not only teaches parts of the body, but you can splash around while you sing.

> *You put your right foot in.*
>   *(put your foot under the water)*
> *You take your right foot out.*
>   *(take your foot out of the water)*
> *You put your right foot in.*
>   *(put your foot back into the water)*
> *And you shake it all about.*
>   *(wiggle your foot back and forth in the water)*
> *Then you do the hokey cokey,*
> *And you turn yourself around.*
>   *(turn your child around in the water)*
> *That's what it's all about.*

◆ Sing other songs that you and your child know.

WHAT YOUR TODDLER WILL LEARN:
Bonding

Jack and Jill

◆ This game will make dressing more fun.

◆ Sit on the floor with your legs straight out. Sit your baby on your knees facing you. Recite this familiar nursery rhyme:

> *Jack and Jill went up the hill,*
> *To fetch a pail of water.*
> *Jack fell down and broke his crown,*
> *And Jill came tumbling after.*

◆ On the word "up", bring your knees up. On the word "down", bring your knees down.

◆ On the word "crown", touch your toddler's head. On "tumbling after", give your toddler a big hug.

WHAT YOUR TODDLER WILL LEARN:
Language skills

Clap the bubble

◆ Playing with bubbles develops many skills in young children. Here are several activities for you to try.

◆ Blow bubbles for your toddler while she is in the bath.

◆ Show your toddler how to keep a bubble in the air by blowing from underneath.

◆ Encourage your toddler to catch a bubble with dry hands, then with wet hands.

◆ Try to pop the bubble by clapping your hands together.

◆ See whether your toddler can pop the bubble by poking a finger through it.

WHAT YOUR TODDLER WILL LEARN:
Hand–eye coordination

Diddle, diddle, dumpling

◆ Undressing your toddler can be fun if you allow plenty of time.

◆ Toddlers usually first show interest in their shoes. Loosen the laces and pull the shoe over his heel, so he only has to pull it off the toes.

◆ Take off socks the same way.

◆ Encourage your toddler to do as much for himself as he can. As he learns to take off shoes and socks, help him to find words to describe his actions. This poem will teach him:

> *Diddle, diddle, dumpling, my son John,*
> *Went to bed with his stockings on.*
> *One shoe off and one shoe on,*
> *Diddle, diddle, dumpling, my son John.*

WHAT YOUR TODDLER WILL LEARN:

Independence

The swimming doll

◆ Get a rubber doll, if possible, with moveable arms and feet.

◆ Let your toddler teach the doll to swim.

◆ Show her how to move the doll's arms and legs.

◆ Give her directions on ways to move the doll in the water, for example, splashing, kicking, shaking.

◆ As your toddler makes her doll swim, recite this rhyme:

> *Swim, swim, little doll*
> *All around the tub.*
> *Splishy splashy, splishy splashy,*
> *Glub, glub, glub.*

WHAT YOUR TODDLER WILL LEARN:

Body awareness

What are you wearing?

◆ Dressing is a wonderful bonding time.

◆ While you dress your child, talk about the colour of his clothes.

◆ Recite this poem about clothes.

> *Mary has a jumper,*
> *And it is blue.*
> *Mary has a jumper,*
> *And it is... (let your child say "blue")*
> *Larry has a shirt,*
> *And it is white.*
> *Larry has a shirt,*
> *And it is... (let your child say "white")*

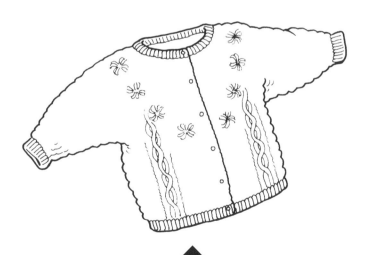

WHAT YOUR TODDLER WILL LEARN:
Language skills

Here is the sea

◆ Recite this poem with your toddler, performing the
actions:

> Here is the sea, the wavy sea,
>   (move both your hands in a wavy pattern)
> Here is my boat,
>   (make a boat with your hands)
> And here is me.
>   (point to yourself)
> All of the fishes down below,
>   (point down)
> Wiggle their tails,
>   (swim your hands around)
> And AWAY they go!
>   (quickly move your hands behind your back)

WHAT YOUR TODDLER WILL LEARN:
Coordination

I brush my teeth

◆ This is a game to teach your toddler about taking care of herself.

> *I brush my teeth in the morning,*
> *I brush my teeth in the morning,*
> *I brush my teeth in the morning,*
> *Every single day.*

◆ Recite the poem while pretending to brush your teeth. Help your toddler pretend to brush her teeth.

◆ With each verse, recite and mime the actions:

> *I comb my hair…*
> *I wash my face…*
> *I wash my hands…*
> *I drink my milk…*

◆ Make up your own verses about the things that you do each day.

WHAT YOUR TODDLER WILL LEARN:
Independence

Sink or float

◆ Baths are always a fun time for your child to experiment with things that sink or float.

◆ Gather together several objects like sponges, inflated balloons, straws, plastic bottles, etc.

◆ Taking one item at a time, say to your child, "Will it sink or will it float?"

◆ Give it to your child to put into the water. Then ask, "Did it sink or did it float?" She will soon understand what the words mean.

◆ Another good toy for the bath is a ping-pong ball. Give the ball to your toddler and see if she can keep it under the water. It's not easy to do and it's always fun when the ball pops up.

WHAT YOUR TODDLER WILL LEARN:
Thinking skills

Finger and Toe Games

Puzzle fun

◆ Select biscuit cutters with shapes such as animals or Christmas trees that your child understands and enjoys.

◆ Press a biscuit cutter into a piece of styrofoam (pizza packaging is great). Use a separate piece of Styrofoam for each biscuit cutter. NOTE: you will need to take care that your child does not put a piece of Styrofoam in her mouth.

◆ Carefully cut around the outline and remove the cutout, keeping the Styrofoam frame intact. Give the cutout to your toddler and show her how to fit it back into the Styrofoam.

◆ Lay all the pieces and cutouts on a table and watch your child concentrate deeply as she matches them.

◆ Once your toddler easily matches all the cutouts, try making several cutouts in a larger piece of Styrofoam.

WHAT YOUR TODDLER WILL LEARN:
To put puzzles together

Watch it fall

◆ Once your child has learned to grasp objects, he must learn to release them.

◆ Sitting in the high chair is a good place from which to watch things fall.

◆ Give your toddler several things to pick up and drop, varying their weight and size.

◆ Try feathers, plastic lids, blocks, ping-pong balls and toys that make sounds when dropped.

◆ This game will encourage your child to release objects.

WHAT YOUR TODDLER WILL LEARN:
Hand release skills

Piggy wig

◆ Recite this rhyme, acting out the story with your hands:

> *Piggy wig and piggy wee*
> > *(hold up your right and left index fingers)*
> *Were hungry as two pigs could be.*
> > *(rub your stomach)*
> *When the farmer called they scurried off,*
> > *(move your index fingers back and forth)*
> *And jumped right in the dinner trough.*
> > *(make a diving motion with both hands)*
>
> *Piggy wig and piggy wee*
> > *(hold up your index fingers)*
> *Were playful as two pigs could be.*
> > *(wiggle your fingers)*
> *They rolled and rolled in the mud all day,*
> > *(roll your hands over each other)*
> *Then went to sleep in the new mown hay.*
> > *(place your hands palm to palm at the side of your head and close your eyes)*

◆ Repeat the rhyme and guide your toddler's hands through the actions.

◆ Soon your toddler will be able to imitate you.

WHAT YOUR TODDLER WILL LEARN:
Imitation

Foxy's hole

◆ Set your toddler on your lap or face him sitting on the floor.

◆ Close your hand into a fist and tell your child that "Foxy's hole" is inside.

◆ Guide your child's finger between the middle fingers of your clenched fist.

◆ Next, open your hand and say, "Foxy's not at home! Foxy's out in the garden, chewing on a bone."

◆ Pretend to chew on your toddler's finger.

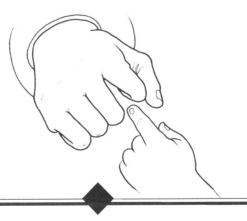

WHAT YOUR TODDLER WILL LEARN:
Language skills

See the little spider

◆ This fingerplay lets you and your toddler share some fun. Walk your fingers along his arms and legs like a crawling spider.

> *See the little spider climbing up the wall.*
> *(walk your fingers slowly up your child's arm)*
> *See the little spider stumble and fall.*
> *(walk your fingers quickly down your child's arm)*
> *See the little spider tumble down the street.*
> *(walk your fingers down your child's leg)*
> *See the little spider stop at your feet.*
> *(stop at your child's feet)*

WHAT YOUR TODDLER WILL LEARN:

Fun

Finger talk

◆ This is a good game to play while waiting at the doctor's or similar places.

◆ Draw faces on your fingers.

◆ Wiggle your fingers back and forth like puppets talking.

◆ Changing the tone and tempo of your voice will delight your child.

◆ The finger puppets can give directions, ask questions and even sing songs.

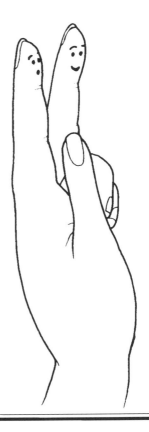

WHAT YOUR TODDLER WILL LEARN:
Language skills

Finger and toe copy game

◆ Play this game with your toddler and at least one other person.

◆ Choose one person to be the leader. Everyone else sits opposite the leader, including you with your child on your lap.

◆ The leader's job is to perform a simple action with his fingers or toes that everyone else can imitate.

◆ As everyone imitates the leader, encourage your toddler to do so, too.

◆ Name the person you are imitating: "Daddy is wiggling his finger," or, "Susie is wiggling her finger."

◆ Guide your toddler through the actions until he can perform them alone.

◆ With fingers or toes, also try wiggling, rolling in a circular motion, moving in a grasping motion, shaking or holding stiff, then relaxing and hitting together.

WHAT YOUR TODDLER WILL LEARN:
Imitation

See my fingers

◆ Sit your toddler in your lap as you recite this poem:

> *See my fingers dance and play.*
> *Fingers dance for me today.*
> *See my ten toes dance and play.*
> *Ten toes dance for me today.*

◆ Touch your child's fingers when you mention fingers, and his toes when you mention toes.

◆ Show your child how to move his fingers and toes in different ways: wiggle, shake, cross hands, cross feet, etc.

WHAT YOUR TODDLER WILL LEARN:
Body awareness

Oliver Twist

◆ Recite this rhyme while you act out the movements, touching your toddler's body as each part is mentioned:

Oliver Twist, Twist, Twist,
Can do this, this, this.
Touch his knees, knees, knees,
Touch his nose, nose, nose,
Touch his hair, hair, hair,
Touch his toes, toes, toes.

Oliver Twist, Twist, Twist,
Can do this, this, this.
Touch his ears, ears, ears,
Touch his waist, waist, waist,
Touch his eyes, eyes, eyes,
Touch his face, face, face.

WHAT YOUR TODDLER WILL LEARN:

Body awareness

Jack-in-the-box

◆ Play this finger exercise with your toddler. Open your hands and wiggle your fingers. Close your hands tightly. Repeat several times.

◆ Close your hands with your thumb tucked inside your fist. Show your child how to do this. You may have to insert his thumb into his fist yourself.

◆ Recite this poem.

> *Jack-in-the-box,*
> *You sit so still.*
>   *(close your hand with your thumb inside)*
> *Won't you come out?*
> *Yes, I will.*
>   *(pop out your thumb)*

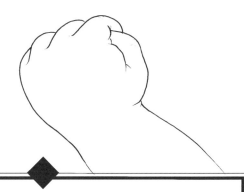

WHAT YOUR TODDLER WILL LEARN:
Coordination

Watch out bunny

◆ Recite this rhyme while you and your toddler carry out the actions:

> *Here is a bunny sitting in the sun.*
>   *(hold up your index and middle fingers like rabbit ears)*
> *Along came a little dog,*
>   *(say, "woof, woof, woof")*
> *Watch that bunny run!*
>   *(make your two fingers hop up your arm like a rabbit running away)*

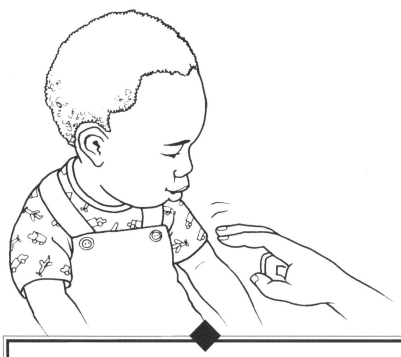

WHAT YOUR TODDLER WILL LEARN:

Imitation

Tommy thumbs

◆ Recite this poem while you and your toddler dance your thumbs as directed:

> *Tommy thumbs up.*
> *Tommy thumbs down.*
> *Tommy thumbs dancing,*
> *All around the town.*
> *Dance them on your shoulders,*
> *Dance them on your head,*
> *Dance them on your knees,*
> *And tuck them into bed.*

◆ On the last line, hide your thumbs behind your back.

◆ Repeat the poem using your index finger:

> *Peter pointer up…*

◆ Repeat, using all your fingers:

> *Finger family up…*

WHAT YOUR TODDLER WILL LEARN:
Imitation

Ten fingers

◆ Sit facing your toddler as you recite this poem, acting out the lines with your fingers:

> *I have ten little fingers,*
> *And they all belong to me.*
> *I can make them do things.*
> *Would you like to see?*
> *I can shut them up tight,*
> *Or open them wide.*
> *I can put them together,*
> *Or make them all hide.*
> *I can make them jump high.*
> *I can make them jump low.*
> *I can fold them quietly.*
> *And hold them just so.*

◆ Repeat the poem and guide your toddler's hands through the actions.

◆ Repeat the poem again and encourage your child to act out the lines with you.

WHAT YOUR TODDLER WILL LEARN:

To follow directions

Tap our legs together

◆ Act out this simple rhyme with your toddler:

> *Let's tap our legs together,*
> *Let's tap our legs together,*
> *Let's tap our legs together,*
> *Every single day.*

◆ Try repeating the rhyme, substituting various actions:

> *Let's wave our hands together…*
> *Let's shake our feet together…*
> *Let's touch our nose together…*
> *Let's clap our hands together…*
> *Let's stretch up high together…*
> *Let's bend down low together…*
> *Let's nod our heads together…*

WHAT YOUR TODDLER WILL LEARN:
Coordination

Biscuit tin

◆ Act out this poem with your hands while you recite. Encourage your toddler to imitate your actions.

> *Here is a biscuit tin.*
>   *(form a circle with your hands, thumbs and*
>   *middle fingers touching)*
> *Here is the lid.*
>   *(stretch your palms flat and parallel to the floor)*
> *Here are the biscuits*
>   *(form circles with your fingers)*
> *That* _____ *[your child's name] likes,*
>   *(pretend to eat the biscuits)*
> *Yum, yum, yum, yum.*

◆ Talk about different kinds of biscuits: oatmeal, chocolate chip, sugar, etc.

◆ Play the game again, but when you say, "Here are the biscuits," substitute the name of the biscuit: "Here are the oatmeal biscuits," for example.

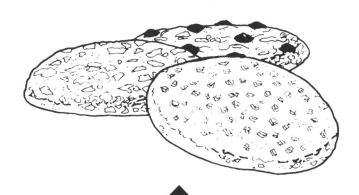

◆

WHAT YOUR TODDLER WILL LEARN:
Imitation

Hand games

◆ When a young child plays games that involve her hands and fingers, she exercises the muscles so important to later development.

◆ Here are easy ways for her to play and exercise her muscles at the same time:

- Wiggle your fingers downwards like rain falling.
- Make circles with your fingers and hold them in front of your eyes like binoculars.
- Move your fingers as if they were paintbrushes.
- Paint circles on your toddler's cheeks, a line down her nose and a dab on her chin.
- Pound your fist, then clap your hands. Each makes a different sound. Alternate them or create patterns like pound, clap; pound, pound, clap, clap; pound, clap, clap; etc.
- Snap your hands open like popcorn popping.
- Open and close your thumb and index finger to "snap baby's nose".

WHAT YOUR TODDLER WILL LEARN:
Fun

A silly song

◆ Sing to the tune of "Row, row, row your boat" and act out the words with your toddler.

> *Clap, clap, clap your hands,*
> *Clap them, 1, 2, 3.*
> *Clap, clap, clap your hands,*
> *And point your finger at me!*

◆ Substitute other actions in the song, and repeat the game. For example:

- shake your hands,
- roll your fists,
- wiggle your fingers,
- rub your hands,
- stamp your feet,
- wiggle your nose,
- pound your fist,
- blink your eyes.

WHAT YOUR TODDLER WILL LEARN:
Fun

I touch

◆ While you recite this rhyme, use your fingers to touch the parts of the body named:

> *I touch my fingers,*
> *I touch my toes,*
> *I touch my ears,*
> *And I touch my nose.*
> *I touch my eyes,*
> *They are open very wide.*
> *I touch my mouth,*
> *With teeth inside.*

◆ Use your toes to act out this rhyme:

> *I touch my ankle,*
> *I touch my knee,*
> *I touch my tummy for all to see.*
> *I touch my fingers,*
> *I touch my cheek,*
> *I touch my nose,*
> *Every day of the week.*

◆ While you repeat the rhymes, show your toddler how to touch the parts of her body with her fingers and toes.

WHAT YOUR TODDLER WILL LEARN:
Body awareness

Butterfly

◆ Talk about butterflies with your child. Go outside and look for butterflies to observe.

◆ Connect your thumbs and wave your fingers like a butterfly.

◆ Fly the butterfly around while you recite this rhyme:

> *Butterfly, butterfly, 'round and 'round you fly,*
> *Swaying, swaying, gently in the sky.*
> *Where will you land when you stop?*
> *I know … . Here!*

◆ Land the butterfly on your toddler's nose.

◆ Repeat the poem and help your toddler wave his hands like a butterfly and land on your nose. This may not be easy for your child to do by himself.

WHAT YOUR TODDLER WILL LEARN:
Listening skills

Index